PARENTING
IN THE
AGE OF MCDONALD'S

Tanuja Sodhi is a well-known diet and fitness consultant and a marathoner with numerous podium finishes. Her exposure to a physically rigorous lifestyle began in the armed forces—where she was part of the pioneering batch of women officers in the Indian navy. She attributes her fine health and terrific fitness to her stint in the defence forces.

Subsequently, Tanuja secured a fellowship in applied nutrition from Medvarsity, Hyderabad and a Reebok certification in fitness. She also holds an MBA (HR) from Jamnalal Bajaj Institute of Management, Mumbai and a Master's degree in English. Tanuja has a number of blogs on nutrition and fitness to her credit.

For more information, contact her at tanujasodhi@gmail.com or visit www.tanujasodhi.com

PARENTING
IN THE
AGE OF MCDONALD'S
Raising the Fast-Food Generation

TANUJA SODHI

RUPA

Published by
Rupa Publications India Pvt. Ltd 2016
7/16, Ansari Road, Daryaganj
New Delhi 110002

Sales centres:
Allahabad Bengaluru Chennai
Hyderabad Jaipur Kathmandu
Kolkata Mumbai

ISBN: 978-81-291-3772-2

First impression 2016

10 9 8 7 6 5 4 3 2 1

The moral right of the author has been asserted.

To my parents,
Vyas and Kunti
for making me who I am today

Contents

Contents

Introduction

I slammed the door behind me as I rushed out of my paediatrician's clinic, tears rolling down my cheeks. Disbelief was writ large on my face. Could I have been so naive to have completely missed the writing on the wall? Yes, I had been oblivious to the obvious—and that made me feel like a complete feather-brain! The bubble of my blissful delusion had just been ruthlessly burst by the doctor when he pronounced my son as 'OBESE'! That was not all. He reprimanded me for regularly 'over-stuffing' my hapless baby till his little stomach revolted in protest. Just to give you the background: I had taken my four-year-old son to the doctor since he suffered from an upset tummy ever so often. No marks for guessing what the cause was! The doctor opened my unheeding eyes to the perils of raising an obese child when he rattled off a list of maladies that a child could be prone to early in life, such as diabetes, high blood pressure, high cholesterol and low self-esteem. The list sounded alarmingly bleak.

This was way back in 2001 and now at seventeen years, Angad stands lean and muscular without the tell-tale signs of the blubber that cushioned him. Today, I can claim to be a proactively clued-in mother who has read extensively and changed how I handled the health of my child. It was the deep fear of the dire consequences of obesity that had hit me really hard and jolted me out of my cosy stupor.

Even in this day and age, when there is a tsunami of information swamping the Internet and print media, there are enough parents who play it by ear. They still believe in many moth-eaten practices that have lost their relevance in today's world. For them, their overweight child may mean a healthy *'khate peete ghar ka bachcha'* (a well-fed child from a well-heeled family), who needs a daily dose of two big glasses of full-fat milk, big dollops of butter on toasts and desi ghee on aloo paranthas to maintain his 'ruddy health'. (I perfectly fit into this slot back then).

Then there is another league of parents. These parents are obsessively anxious about their children's health, going overboard to squash an 'imminent ailment' even before it dares to draw near their little ones. They fill the kids with countless supplements to 'fortify' their health. They go to extremes to banish the word 'junk' (read 'ultimate pleasure-giving foods') from their household, as if it were a deadly virus. Little do they know that it's just fine to pander to the little ones' pleas for food indulgences once in a while, so that they do not feel deprived when they longingly look at other kids chowing down their 'comfort foods' with great exuberance. Occasional nutritional aberrations keep children from rebelling against an overly rigid dietary regime, as total denial can make them feel that they're missing out on all the goodies, leading to unrestrained consumption of unhealthy favourites on the sly.

Not to forget the batch of ever-confused parents who look up websites online to solve all their parental woes and come back more baffled than ever before, as the Internet has a wicked reputation of contradicting just about everything it proclaims. One has to be conversant with the authentic internet sites to get relevant advice.

There is quite a lot of substance in what Ed Asner (American hero of yesteryears) had once said, 'Raising kids is part joy and part guerrilla warfare.'

Being a parent is certainly not one of the easiest tasks planned for mankind. It is meant to keep you perpetually on your toes. You may sometimes even consider meeting a shrink (instead of a nutritionist) to help you deal with your young one's food tantrums, as you may start blaming your 'inadequate parenting skills' for the onset of insanity.

On a relatively serious note, this book is for you if any of the following descriptions matches the profile of your child:

Picky eater: You're always running after your child. Trying to make him eat even a single meal successfully is a mission for you. You feel you're off your rocker by the end of every meal, ready to scream your lungs out (in exhilaration if successful, in frustration if it's a disaster as usual).

Overweight child: While you think you have a pleasingly healthy child at home, the world is psyching you to believe otherwise. You dread visiting your child's paediatrician as he rebukes you for overfeeding him, and scares the hell out of you by talking about the risks of obesity.

Underweight child: You think you're feeding your baby enough through the day until she is ready to throw up, but she shows no signs of any horizontal growth. While the world chides you (read neighbours, in-laws, relatives and other random people) for not taking care of her health, the doctor says all is well and she is healthy. You are truly confused about who to believe and what course of action to take.

Young athlete: Your boy is proficient at a sport and is keen on taking it up in a big way. The only problem is that he burns out easily. He often complains of feeling weak and worn down.

This book may serve also as a handbook in any of the following situations that may be a part of your existence:

You have a pre-schooler: Your toddler is ready to start attending pre-school. It's going to be tiffin time for him and you're perplexed at the choices or the lack of them from the nutritional point of view.

Your child's exams are approaching: Your child cannot concentrate for more than thirty minutes while studying. She lacks focus and appears distracted more often than not. You are distressed, trying to figure out where you're going wrong.

You are taking off on a road trip with family: You're scouting for healthy takeaway ideas other than your usual preparations.

Your child is going through growth spurts: You want to accelerate her growth with the right nutrients while she is growing. As usual, there are confusing inputs and tip-offs on how to speed up the process.

Your child is awfully bored with your cooking: You're pretty sure and rightfully worried that the next time you push that uninspiring and predictable platter under her nose, all hell will break loose with 'rebel' writ large on her face. You shudder to think of the scenario and are looking out for healthy yet toothsome options.

You are a first-time mother: Here is your first child and you're as clueless about good nutrition as you are about most other issues concerning him. So, you're scouting for a good handbook on nutrition to help you sail smoothly through your first-time parenthood.

You're a mother to a perfectly healthy child: Well, it may sound bemusing to you but yes, you too, could benefit from the book. There are loads of ideas on healthy eating and exercising in the book that could help you maintain your child's good health.

Apart from the above situations, there could be a whole lot of other frivolous-sounding but true-to-life reasons that may motivate you to opt for the book. These could be:

Your faith in the Internet is wavering: It confuses you no end by giving out conflicting information from a million, authentic and unreliable, sources. The problem is that you're clueless on which ones to trust.

You're an inquisitive mother: You're keen to keep abreast of the latest information on child nutrition.

You'd like a ready-reckoner: You long to own a book on child nutrition that will end your quest for a comprehensive title, that answers all the questions you are likely to have until your baby turns eighteen.

This book is for you if you're NOT looking for a thesis with medical jargon and terminology. You really don't wish to know about the complex technical aspects of nutrition. Reading this book will be akin to learning to drive a car without needing to know about the nitty-gritty of its engine. The book is simple, practical and to the point.

There are other reasons, too, to pick this book—either because you need a gift for a visiting friend/relative (a parent or a would-be parent) and want it to be practical and worthwhile; or you need to kill time at the airport bookstore. Along the way, you discover that this title is so engrossing that you can't do without reading it to the end (Wink, wink!).

Since I have been a mother for the last seventeen years and a nutritionist who has interacted with a slew of clients to date, I have ensured that the book is replete with real-life experiences and instances from different stages of my journey as a mother and a nutritionist. I have gleaned priceless information and insights from the lives of my friends, my diet clients, my fitness clients and the mothers of my son's friends.

This book has been shaped on the basis of the 'trials and tribulations' of real people, which is one of the unique features of the book. I have attempted to keep it light yet insanely useful!

Besides the content-based relevance of the book, you will find it appealing for its simple, breezy style of writing that makes it a remarkably easy read. Due to this simplicity, the book reassuringly does not qualify as a sleeping pill that lulls the senses of the readers, transporting them to slumberland. The book does not go into the boring brass tacks of dietetics, as mentioned earlier. Instead, it guides you in the most uncomplicated manner, assuming you're a non-medical mortal disinterested in the science and maths behind various recommendations.

If you're not a fast reader and think it is worthless buying a book since you're unlikely to ever read it from start to finish, then here's the deal-sealer for you. Each chapter in the book is *independent* of the rest of the book and not sequentially arranged in any way. This will allow you to skip some topics and zoom-in straight to the chapters of your interest, without the burden of reading each and every written word.

I have consciously adhered to imparting very practical and doable diet tips. The recommendations are tailored to fit our kids in the Indian scenario, with situations that are typically Indian and thus, relevant. In the same spirit, the ingredients of all the recipes in this book are easily available in local departmental stores, with most of them being a part of day-to-day cooking. I have even endeavoured to source recipes from mothers in my friends' circle, my young clients' mothers and mothers/aunts who are cooking aficionados.

The objective of this book is to help parents strengthen the nutritional foundation of their children. It is a herculean task for full-grown adults to unlearn the unhealthy eating habits and embrace the healthy ones. It is much easier to build healthy habits while children are very young and impressionable. This solid dietary foundation carries forward into adulthood and the momentum continues. So, the idea is to *catch 'em young* and see them blossom into fit and healthy adults.

Let's prove P.J.O'Rourke (American journalist and writer) wrong when he says, 'Everybody knows how to raise children, except the people who have them.'

Chapter 1

A Goulash of Good Health

A Balanced Diet

Aeons ago, when we were kids, 'special' foods could be counted on fingertips. There really wasn't a cartful of epicurean delights to spoil us silly. Perhaps the term 'junk food' was not even conceived since the huge junk-pile of these foods in today's age barely existed. It's raining burgers, pizzas, French fries, cookies, doughnuts, sodas, chips and a great deal more nowadays. The list keeps growing endlessly.

Though there would be occasional 'not-really-healthy' treats in the form of deep-fried homemade pakodas, chhole bhature, halwa poori, papads and so on, they would be lost like a needle in a haystack in the glut of banefully-unhealthy fast foods available today. As kids, we would burn off the calories with our physical alacrity, as stepping out of the house to play was a much-awaited treat every evening. Nobody had to shove us out of the house, pestering us to go out and play! Today's kids are pretty much glued to gadgets, perpetually holed up inside four walls. The likely fall-out? Obesity, diabetes, heart ailments, hypertension, bone pain due to lack of vitamin D and other lifestyle diseases.

To add fuel to the already raging fire, aggressive marketing by the food and beverage industry with its slurp-worthy food visuals, is luring the kids like crazy. These ubiquitous junk foods have cast such an evil spell on the psyche of the young children that parents are often forced to surrender helplessly to the will of their little and not-so-little brats for peace in the house.

While many parents today are wised-up on what is good for their kids, many mums and dads still remain flummoxed. As a first-time mother, I too, was clueless about the balanced diet concept until I read extensively on the topic and researched it. Therefore, I can relate to baffled parents ready with a barrage of questions about the diet of their children. Some of these queries are:

- ❑ Why is my little girl lethargic and listless all day?
- ❑ Will my son ever put on weight on his bony frame?
- ❑ Is my child getting the nutrients that she needs to grow tall?
- ❑ Are all fats bad for my little one?

These are some of the top-of-the-list worries gnawing at parents' minds when their kids are of a growing age. While kids come in many different shapes and sizes, growing at their individual rates, we as parents can contribute significantly to their growth by administering good nutrition. The pay-off? A child with a healthy weight, strong bones and teeth, an efficient digestive system and a robust immune system.

Keeping in mind these common apprehensions that plague today's parents, I have laid out the details of healthy and crucial nutrients in a balanced diet that help the child's body to optimize its growth mechanism and help maintain sterling health all through the growing years.

A balanced diet for children provides essential macronutrients and micronutrients that they need for healthy growth and development.

The much-touted 'Eatwell Plate' is a very handy tool that can help you to plan your child's diet in a very basic manner simply by glancing at the proportions of each nutrient displayed in it. It is a very simple categorization of nutrients where a single visual representation can clear fundamental doubts about the proportion of important nutrients given below. Let's scrutinize each one of them.

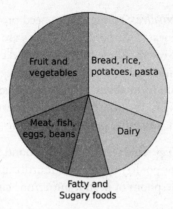

Fruits and vegetables: Powerhouses of vitamins and minerals, fruits and vegetables should form around 33 per cent of your child's daily diet. It's a healthy practice to eat at least five portions or servings of a variety of fruit and vegetables every day.

Examples of servings: half a cup of raw or cooked vegetables/one cup of cooked leafy vegetables/one small potato/one medium carrot/half a cup of broccoli make a single serving of vegetables.

One cup of chopped mixed fruits/one medium apple or pear or banana or orange/one cup diced watermelon or papaya or muskmelon/ half a cup of dried fruit make a serving of fruit.

Breads, cereals, potatoes and other starchy foods: These foods, which are essentially carbohydrates, should also make up around 33 per cent of your child's daily intake. They provide energy to the young and restless. Try to pick high-fibre carbohydrates like whole grains and wholewheat pasta.

Examples of servings: one slice of bread/ half a cup of cooked rice/half a cup of cooked pasta/one cup of ready-to-eat cereal are single servings.

Meat, fish and alternatives: Young bodies need protein for growth and repair. So, meat, fish, poultry and eggs are rich sources of protein for meat-eaters. These foods are also excellent source of vitamins and minerals like B_{12}, iron and omega-3 fatty acids. This group should form about 12 per cent of your child's daily diet. For vegetarians, the non-dairy protein alternatives are dals, dried beans, tofu, soy milk, peanut butter, nuts and seeds.

Examples of servings: One serving equals around 28 to 30 grams of cooked meat or poultry or fish/one-fourth cup cooked beans/ one egg/two tablespoons of peanut butter/one cup soy milk/one cup dal.

Milk and dairy foods: Milk and dairy foods are excellent sources of protein and should form about 15 per cent of your child's daily diet. They are also packed with calcium, potassium and magnesium, which are essential for bone health. However, go for the low-fat variety.

Examples of servings: one cup of milk/one cup of yogurt/50 grams of cheese make for a serving of dairy foods.

Fatty and sugary foods: Though fats and sugary foods are both energy-providing foods, they're high on calories. Excessive consumption of these foods can topple the 'calorie input vs calorie output' equilibrium in the body, leading to unneeded weight gain. This food group is also the main cause of adult-onset diabetes and heart diseases. So, these should be consumed only occasionally and you should choose good fats and natural sugar sources as discussed at length later in this book. This group should not exceed 7 per cent of your child's daily intake.

Examples of servings: one handful of nuts/one to two tablespoons of oil depending upon age, gender and activity levels.

The 'Eatwell Plate' is undoubtedly a good start-point for the uninitiated. But as a discerning parent, you need to delve deeper for information on healthy nutrition rather than just getting 'a fair idea' about the nutritional needs of your kids. To do so, you need a deeper insight well beyond the bounds of these five broad categories.

Parents who want to get to the fundamentals of their children's diet so that they know the implication of every bite and sip that passes through their little food pipes, need to understand essential nutrients such as carbohydrates, proteins, fats, vitamins, minerals, roughage and water. To help deconstruct them, they have been further categorized as macronutrients, micronutrients and other essential nutrients.

Macronutrients are nutrients like carbohydrates, proteins and fats, while micronutrients comprise all the vitamins and minerals. The other essential nutrients are dietary roughage (fibre) and hydration (water). We shall also deliberate on fruits and vegetables in a separate chapter as these nutrients are critical to the general health of children.

Calorie Grids

Here are the two grids displaying the calorie needs of children according to their age groups and activity levels. At one glance, parents can get a fair idea about how to provide a balance of nutrients to their children through their daily diet.

Girls

Age	Calories (Kcals per day)		
	Sedentary	*Moderately Active*	*Active*
0–6 months		650	
7–12 months		850–900	
2–3 years	1000	1000–1400	1000–1400
4–8 years	1200	1400–1600	1400–1800
9–13 years	1600	1600–2000	1800–2200
14–18 years	1800	2000	2400

Age	Protein (grams per day)	Carbohydrates (per day)	Fats (per day)
0–6 months	9	60 grams	31 grams
7–12 months	11	95 grams	30 grams
2–3 years	13	45–65% of total Kcals	30–40% of total Kcals
4–8 years	19	45–65% of total Kcals	25–35% of total Kcals
9–13 years	34	45–65% of total Kcals	25–35% of total Kcals
14–18 years	46	45–65% of total Kcals	25–35% of total Kcals

Age	Dairy (cups per day)	Fruits (cups per day)	Vegetables (cups per day)
0–6 months	N/A	N/A	N/A
7–12 months	One-third	One-fourth to half	One-fourth to half
2–3 years	2–2.5	1–1.5	1–1.5
4–8 years	2.5–3	1–1.5	1.5–2.5
9–13 years	2.5–3	1.5–2	1.5–3
14–18 years	3	1.5–2	2.5–3

Boys

Age	Calories (Kcals per day)		
	Sedentary	*Moderately Active*	*Active*
0–6 months		650	
7–12 months		850–900	
2–3 years	1000	1000–1400	1000–1400
4–8 years	1400	1400–1600	1600–2000
9–13 years	1800	1800–2200	2000–2600
14–18 years	2200	2400–2800	2800–3200

Age	Protein (grams per day)	Carbohydrates (per day)	Fats (per day)
0–6 months	9	60 grams	31 grams
7–12 months	11	95 grams	30 grams
2–3 years	13	45–65% of total Kcals	30–40% of total Kcals
4–8 years	19	45–65% of total Kcals	25–35% of total Kcals
9–13 years	34	45–65% of total Kcals	25–35% of total Kcals
14–18 years	52	45–65% of total Kcals	25–35% of total Kcals

Age	Dairy (cups per day)	Fruits (cups per day)	Vegetables (cups per day)
0–6 months	N/A	N/A	N/A
7–12 months	One-third	One-fourth to half	One-fourth to half
2–3 years	2–2.5	1–1.5	1–1.5
4–8 years	2.5–3	1–2	1.5–2.5
9–13 years	3	1.5–2	2–3.5
14–18 years	3	2–2.5	2.5–4

The Verdict

Our efforts are an investment in the strong and healthy adulthood of our children. Keep offering a variety of nutritious foods to your little ones to make them a part of their balanced diet. With small changes in the diet, you can get the kids into the habit of eating wholesome food. In this way, you can set the tone for a lifetime of healthy eating. So, clear your kitchen cabinet of all chips, cookies and soda, and train your entire family to eat healthy.

So, what have you planned for dinner tonight? Nothing yet? Pull yourself up, mix and match from the listed nutrients, smile with your newly acquired confidence (with wisdom comes confidence!) and dish up the nutritious goodies. Then watch your child grow healthier with each passing day!

Chapter 2

The Incredibles 1

Macronutrients

Macronutrients can be described as energy-providing chemical substances consumed by humans in large quantities. In this chapter, I will describe each one of these essential components of a balanced diet. The three macronutrients are carbohydrates, proteins and fats. When you're planning the daily diet of your child, you cannot overlook this crucial trio, the bedrock of a balanced diet. Imagine a diet without roti, bread, rice, eggs, vegetables, fruits, milk and meat! Absurd, isn't it? Such is the dominance of these three big guns in the area of nutrition. So, let's get introduced to each of them to understand their individual worth.

Carbohydrates

The body's main source of fuel, carbohydrates are used by the body to burn calories and get energy. Children get plenty of exercise by playing rigorous games, sports and running around the whole day and, therefore, need a considerable amount of carbs to refuel their young bodies. Carbs are also crucial for the central nervous system, the kidneys, the brain, the muscles and the heart to function efficiently.

Beauty and the Beast

Good carbohydrates (complex carbs): These provide ample fibre to the body and, therefore, get absorbed slowly into the body. Roughage creates a feeling of satiety and thus, control cravings caused by blood-sugar spikes.

The list of worthy carbs includes wholewheat/multigrain

bread; wholewheat flour/multigrain roti and brown rice. It also includes breakfast cereals such as oatmeal, oat bran, broken wheat porridge, unsweetened wheat flakes or muesli without artificial fruits or added sugar.

Whole grains such as wholewheat, bran, soya, pearl millet, cracked wheat, quinoa, buckwheat, amaranth, barley, sorghum and chana are recommended.

So are lentils and legumes, including all dried beans like kidney beans, black beans, garbanzo beans, black-eyed beans, black chana, dried peas, navy beans, dals, sprouts and so on.

Other items in this list are wholewheat pasta; fibrous vegetables like potato, sweet potato, beans and peas; and fibrous fruits like apple, pear and avocado.

Bad carbohydrates (simple carbs): These are refined or processed carbohydrates that come without the all-essential fibre. Minimize your child's health risk by eliminating or drastically reducing these simple carbs from the diet. Too much consumption of these items could cause obesity in children and adult-onset diabetes.

Commonly eaten simple carbohydrates are white bread; white rice; refined flour and its products; and breakfast cereals like fruit loops, chocolate or honey-based flakes/loops, muesli with dehydrated fruits, sugary cornflakes, candied crisps and nuts, frosted flakes, chocolate or honey-coated puffed rice.

Other culprits are pasta made with refined flour; beverages like fizzy drinks, fruit drinks, energy drinks, flavoured water, heavy milkshakes sweetened with excess sugar or chocolate syrup; and all foods with simple added sugars like cakes, doughnuts, pastries, cookies, candies, Indian sweets and chocolates.

Refined grains are processed to remove the bran and germ. Although this gives a finer texture to the grain, it also gets rid of the dietary fibre, iron and many B vitamins, making it less nutritious. Since whole grains contain the complete grain kernel with the bran, germ and endosperm, they are rich in dietary fibre, vitamins and minerals.

Proteins

Essential for the growth of children, proteins are the building blocks for bones, muscles, tissues, cartilage, skin and blood in your child's body. In fact, protein is an important component of every cell in the body. It is needed for the immune system to function efficiently, to build and repair tissues, as a secondary energy source and to make enzymes and hormones. A child's body needs relatively large amount of proteins, primarily to aid in overall growth.

Beauty and the Beast

Lean proteins: Always serve a variety of lean proteins as these are low in saturated fats that raise the levels of bad cholesterol.

Food items recommended within this category are chicken breasts without skin (baked, boiled, grilled); low-fat dairy (milk, curd, paneer, cheese and buttermilk); eggs; fish and seafood (baked, boiled, grilled); and soy products such as tofu, soy milk, soybeans, soy nuggets, soy granules and soy flour.

Also worth mentioning are dried beans and lentils such as dals, kidney beans, black beans, garbanzo beans, black-eyed beans, black chana, dried peas and navy beans; nuts like almonds, pistachios, walnuts, cashews, Brazil nuts, pine nuts and hazelnuts; seeds of pumpkin, sunflower, chia seeds and flaxseeds; and of course, quinoa.

For healthy children of reasonable weight, low-fat dairy products are sufficient. Also, cashews and Brazil nuts may be good sources of protein, but are high in saturated fats and therefore, should be consumed in moderation.

Unhealthy proteins: These are high on saturated fats, which are harmful for the heart, raising the risk of heart disease. The culprits include frozen/ready-to-eat/processed meats like sausages, salami, fried chicken, fried fish fingers; full-fat dairy products like milk, curd, creamy cheese, creamy cottage cheese; and red meat like mutton, beef and pork.

Eating foods which are high in saturated fats can spike the levels of bad cholesterol (LDL) in the blood, causing the formation of plaque in the arteries in adulthood.

Protein from animal sources is the actual home of all the essential amino acids that children need, while plant sources of protein do not contain all of the essential amino acids. But an excessive amount of meat can also be counterproductive, as it can put children at the risk of illnesses such as heart disease, kidney disease and cancer.

Fats

The very word 'fat' conjures up images of a huge girth and a tubby body in our minds. Fat has earned a nasty reputation over a period of time. The common misconception is that all fat is bad and causes unnecessary weight gain, but you must know that all fats are not the same. There is the good fat and the evil fat. Some amount of fat is essential for our body's sustenance.

Fat is essential for the normal growth and development of the body because it helps vitamin A, D, E and K to travel through the bloodstream and eventually get absorbed by the body. Fat has a number of other important functions to play such as giving energy to the body; providing protection for the vital organs; supplying insulation for body temperature; and playing a role in brain development, cell membrane maintenance and blood clotting. It is also essential for good skin and for enhancing the taste of food.

Fat is the most concentrated food energy source as compared to carbohydrates and proteins, with nine calories of energy in every gram of fat, more than twice the energy that proteins or carbohydrates provide with their 4 calories each per gram. So, fat can really be a great help for undernourished children.

Beauty and the Beast

Good fats (unsaturated fats): Since children need some dietary fat for the reasons pointed out above, add them to their diet but choose them sensibly. When eaten in moderation, these fats help lower cholesterol levels and reduce the risk of heart disease in adulthood. Good fats are of two kinds: monounsaturated fats and polyunsaturated fats.

These heart-healthy fats can be found in oils such as olive, canola, soybean, corn, peanut, flaxseed, sesame, almond, sunflower and safflower; olives; peanut butter; avocados; nuts like hazelnuts, almonds, walnuts, pistachios, Brazil nuts, cashews and pine nuts; seeds like flaxseeds, sesame and pumpkin; and fatty fish like salmon, tuna, mackerel, catfish, herring, anchovies and trout.

Bad fats (saturated fats and trans fats): These two types of fats are the evil guys that are best left alone. Both can jack up bad cholesterol levels, clog arteries and heighten the risk for heart disease in adulthood.

These two villains are primarily found hiding in full-fat dairy products like butter, cream, cheese, full-fat milk, high-fat cottage cheese (paneer), full-fat curd and clarified butter (ghee).

They're also found in desserts like fruit cream, kheer, halwa and sweetmeats; ice cream and ice cream shakes; milkshakes; egg yolk; hydrogenated oils, palm oil and coconut oil; margarine, shortenings and lard; salad dressings and sandwich spreads such as the Caesar salad dressing, Ranch dressing, Thousand Island dressing, mayonnaise and coleslaw; coconut products; and animal products such as liver, other organ meats, poultry, sausages, salamis, bacon, meat with skin.

The culprits also include most commercially prepared food items such as burgers, pizzas, hotdogs, cakes, doughnuts, chips and cookies; and all deep-fried foods.

Most restaurants prepare food in hydrogenated oils to enhance the flavours. So there! If you care for the heart of the apple of your eyes, you are duty-bound to restrict these foods to 10 per cent or less of her total calorie intake.

In order to promote a healthy weight, trim unnecessary fat from your child's diet by serving her only low-fat dairy products, poultry without skin and lean cuts of meats. Feed nuts in moderation as some of them are high in saturated fat. These are cashew, Brazil nuts, pecans and macadamia.

A word of caution! Don't go overboard even with healthy fats, as fats are much higher in calories compared with other macronutrients such as carbohydrates and proteins.

The Verdict

Macronutrients are the big guys of nutrition. They are the backbone of your child's daily diet. Meddling with their proportions could jeopardize the long-term health of a child, so play it safe with the big players!

Chapter 3
The Incredibles 2
Micronutrients

Will my little girl put on weight on her bony body? Will my boy always remain lethargic and listless or will he be high on energy some day? Is my child getting a good diet that facilitates growth? These are some of the top-of-the-list worries gnawing at parents' minds when their kids are growing up. While kids grow at their individual rates, we as parents can play an important role in their growth by ensuring their nutritional needs are met. The payoff? A child with a healthy weight, strong bones and teeth, a well-regulated digestive system and healthy dietary habits will carry these benefits throughout her life.

While macronutrients such as proteins, carbohydrates and good fats are absolutely vital for the growth and development of our young ones, this growth is incomplete without micronutrients such as vitamins and minerals. Although micronutrients are required only in tiny quantities, they play an indispensable role in healthy and disease-free growth. A deficiency of these nutrients due to an inadequate diet could cause serious health problems in our children.

So, I have laid out the minutiae on ten most crucial nutrients that a growing body needs to develop optimally.

Calcium
Remember the colourful calcium toy-containers that lured kids to gobble up pastel-hued calcium tablets without the customary fuss associated with swallowing pills? Those weren't designed without a purpose. Since calcium is the most important nutrient for growing kids, the flurry around its packaging is not totally

irrelevant. Calcium prevents the bone-robbers from stealing away bone density by strengthening the bones and teeth through the growing years. Calcium in the blood helps maintain the heart rhythm and promotes proper blood clotting and muscular function. Teenagers, especially girls, often get far less calcium than they should. A deficiency in calcium could stunt growth and increase the risk of osteoporosis later in life, when their bodies begin to leach calcium from the bones. So, adequate calcium intake will ensure a sufficiency of bone density in their adulthood.

Recommended quantity of calcium per day

Children 2–3 years	500 mg
Children 4–8 years	800 mg
Children 9–18 years	1,300 mg

Good Sources

Some excellent sources of calcium are dairy products like milk, cheese, curd, cottage cheese (paneer), buttermilk; soy products like tofu, soy milk, soy greens, soybeans, soybean sprouts and soy nuggets; vegetables like broccoli, turnip greens, mustard greens, okra and edamame; and dark green, leafy vegetables such as spinach, kale, bok choy, collard greens.

One can also recommend grains like finger millet, quinoa and wholewheat; bony fish like salmon, sardines, rainbow trout; seeds like sesame seeds, flaxseeds and chia seeds; dried fruits like dried apricots, seedless raisins, dried plums, dried pears, dates and dried figs; nuts like almonds and Brazil nuts; beans such as white beans and soybean; and calcium-fortified foods like cereals and orange juice.

Iron

Don't mess with this mineral. There is just too much at stake if this nutrient is deficient in the body. Iron is body's one of the most precious minerals needed for the formation of haemoglobin.

It helps our body to generate the energy we need to undertake everyday activities. So, not having enough iron in the body can lead to iron-deficiency anaemia, a condition characterized by fatigue, shortness of breath, dizziness, weight loss and headaches. Girls are especially susceptible to iron deficiency at puberty as they start losing more iron through menstruation.

Iron also plays an important role in the development of the brain during the early years, impacting behaviour and intelligence. In children, the consequences of iron deficiency are severe, potentially affecting behaviour and normal intellectual development. It is also vital in strengthening the immune system.

Iron can be absorbed better by the body when consumed with vitamin C (an iron absorption enhancer).

Recommended quantity of iron per day

7–12 months	11 mg
1–3 years	7 mg
4 –8 years	10 mg
9–13 years	8 mg
14–18 years, girls	15 mg
14–18 years, boys	11 mg

Good Sources

Some excellent sources of iron are meats like mutton liver, beef and chicken liver; eggs; oysters; fish like halibut, salmon and tuna; wheat germ; green vegetables like spinach, lima beans, parsley and edamame; dried fruits like raisins, peaches, apricots and prunes; beans like kidney beans, black beans, black-eyed beans, soybeans and chickpeas; lentils (dals); and tofu.

Other recommend food items are whole grains like quinoa, buckwheat, wholewheat, barley, sorghum and oats; wholewheat bread; seeds like pumpkin seeds, sunflower seeds, flaxseeds and sesame seeds; nuts like almonds, walnuts, cashews, pistachios, hazelnuts, pine nuts and peanuts; peanut butter; and fortified cereals.

Vitamin A

Whenever you think of those beautiful eyes, vitamin A should come to your mind. Vitamin A is critical for sharp vision, healthy skin, teeth, bones and immune system, cell growth and for maintenance of vital body organs. There are two forms of vitamin A, namely, retinoid and beta-carotene. While retinoids come from animal products, beta-carotenes come from plant sources.

Vitamin A deficiency can lead to vision problems and increase the likelihood of infections. In extreme cases, the deficiency can lead to blindness.

Recommended quantity of vitamin A per day

Children 1–3 years	300 mcg
Children 4–8 years	400 mcg
Children 9–13 years	600 mcg
Children 14–18 years	900 mcg

Good Sources

Several vegetables are rich sources of Vitamin A, including sweet potato, spinach, red cabbage, pumpkin, squash, carrots, red capsicum, peas, asparagus, beet greens, mustard greens, turnip greens, tomato, Chinese cabbage and parsley. Fruits, too, are recommended, which include muskmelon, mango, apricots, grapefruit, tangerines, papaya, watermelon and guava.

Other sources of vitamin A are meats like beef liver, lamb liver, chicken breast and chicken liver; fish like herring and tuna; cod liver oil; dried beans like black-eyed peas; dairy products like cheddar cheese; eggs; and dried fruits like prunes, peaches and apricots.

Magnesium

Magnesium is our 'jack of all trades' mineral as it plays an important role in almost 300 bodily functions, including those of the muscles, nerves and heart. It keeps the bones and teeth strong and boosts the immune system. Magnesium also helps keep the blood pressure normal and heart rhythm stable. This is not all. This mineral also plays a significant role in blood glucose level control and muscle contraction and relaxation. Many enzymes, which our body need to make energy, can only be activated by magnesium. Finally, magnesium aids in the regulation of other important nutrients such as calcium, copper, zinc, vitamin D and potassium.

Magnesium deficiency can lead to muscle cramps, nausea, anxiety, fatigue, high blood pressure and confusion, to name a few health problems.

Recommended quantity of magnesium per day

Infants up to 3 years	30–80 mg
Children 4–8 years	130 mg
Children 9–13 years	240 mg
Boys 14–18 years	410 mg
Girls 14–18 years	360 mg

Good Sources

Some great sources of magnesium are wheat germ; vegetables like spinach, beet greens, lima beans, edamame beans, potatoes and sweet potato; whole-grain breads and cereals like wholewheat, barley, brown rice, quinoa, bulgur, buckwheat, millet and oats; dried beans and lentils like soybeans, black-eyed peas and chickpeas; and dried fruits like figs.

Also finding a place in this list are seeds like sesame seeds, sunflower seeds, flaxseeds and pumpkin seeds; nuts like almonds, Brazil nuts, hazelnuts, cashew nuts, walnuts, pistachios and peanuts; fish like halibut and mackerel; oysters; peanut butter; and eggs.

Vitamin E

Proud of your daughter's 'peaches and cream' skin that invites a shower of compliments? Give credit to vitamin E that is working through her diet. Vitamin E is a powerful antioxidant that protects cell membranes and bolsters a healthy immune system. It promotes healthy skin, the health of red blood cells and helps the blood to clot during an injury. It fights harmful by-products of everything from air pollution to cigarette smoke to ultraviolet rays. Vitamin E can be sufficiently obtained from dietary sources. A deficiency of vitamin E is rare, but could lead to anaemia.

Recommended quantity of vitamin E per day

Healthy breastfeeding infants 0–6 months	4 mg
Infants 7–12 months	5 mg
Children 1–3 years	6 mg
Children 4–8 years	7 mg
Children 9–13 years	11 mg
Children older than 14 years	15 mg

Good Sources

Fabulous sources of vitamin E include nuts like almonds, Brazil nuts, hazelnuts and peanuts; peanut butter; oils like canola, olive, sunflower, safflower and soybean; vegetables like mustard greens, turnip greens, pumpkin and red peppers; fruits like mangoes and papaya; and sunflower seeds.

Potassium

Potassium is an important electrolyte, the guy who regulates the fluid balance in the blood, thus allowing the cells, tissues and organs to function optimally. It controls the electrical activity of the heart, therefore controlling the heartbeat. Potassium also generates muscle contractions, helps in protein synthesis and metabolizes carbohydrates.

A potassium-rich diet can decrease high blood pressure and may also reduce the risk of kidney stones and bone loss.

Recommended quantity of potassium per day

Babies under 6 months	400 mg
Babies 7 months–1 year	700 mg
Toddlers 1–3 years	3,000 mg
Children 4–8 years	3,800 mg
Children 9–13 years	4,500 mg
Boys and girls over the age of 14	4,700 mg

Good Sources

Here are some great sources of potassium—fruits like banana, avocado and guava; dried fruits like prunes, raisins, figs and peaches; fish like salmon and halibut; vegetables like white potatoes, sweet potato, lima beans, beetroot greens and edamame; nuts like pistachios, hazelnuts, Brazil nuts, peanuts and almonds; dried beans like chickpeas, soybeans and black beans; seeds like sesame seeds, pumpkin seeds, sunflower seeds and flaxseeds; cereals like buckwheat, oats and sorghum; lentils; wheat germ; peanut butter; and lamb liver.

Vitamin C

For the rock-solid immunity of your child, think vitamin C. It is a powerful anti-oxidant that supports the body's immune system and fights cell damage. It is also needed to synthesize collagen, which is essential for the development of healthy skin, bones, gums and blood vessels. Adequate consumption of vitamin C is known to lower the risk of heart stroke in adulthood. It is an accepted remedy for the common cold and helps in wound healing. Vitamin C deficiency can cause scurvy.

Recommended quantity of vitamin C per day

Birth to 6 months	40 mg
Infants 7–12 months	50 mg
Children 1–3 years	15 mg
Children 4–8 years	25 mg
Children 9–13 years	45 mg
Teens 14–18 years (boys)	75 mg
Teens 14–18 years (girls)	65 mg

Good Sources

Dried beans (like kidney beans) and lamb liver are good sources of vitamin C.

Besides these, one can recommend vegetables like broccoli, red cabbage, green capsicum, red capsicum, squash, tomatoes, cauliflower, bok choy, spinach, brussels sprouts, white potatoes, sweet potato, mustard greens, turnip greens, beet greens, peas, cabbage, green beans, pumpkin, parsley, onions and lima beans.

Fruits like orange, grapefruit, strawberries, avocado, lemon, banana, plums, pomegranate, papaya, guava, kiwi, cantaloupe, kiwi, honeydew melon, mango, watermelon, raspberries, pineapple, apricot and Indian gooseberry (amla) are also rich sources.

Vitamin D

Let there be sunshine in your precious one's life and he shall be strong and healthy! Vitamin D is one of the most essential nutrients for strong bones—the sunshine vitamin as it is popularly called. Without a sufficient amount of this super-nutrient, children run the risk of rickets, bone pain, muscle weakness and also fractures and osteoporosis in adulthood. This is largely because vitamin D helps the body to absorb calcium, which is only possible when vitamin D is present in an adequate quantity.

Not just the above, vitamin D helps keep blood pressure from shooting up, it reduces your child's risk of diabetes and lowers her chances of heart attacks and rheumatoid arthritis in adulthood.

Almost 80–90 per cent of this nutrient is obtained through exposure to sunlight. As little as ten to fifteen minutes of sun exposure is sufficient to prevent vitamin D deficiency. It can also be found in small amounts in a very few foods that are listed below.

Recommended quantity of vitamin D per day

Birth to 6 months	200 mg
Infants 7–12 months	260 mg
Children 1–3 years	700 mg
Children 4–8 years	1000 mg
Children 9–18 years	1300 mg

Good Sources

Good sources of vitamin D are cod liver oil; fish like swordfish, halibut, herring, mackerel and sardines; oysters; mushrooms (exposed to ultraviolet rays); egg yolks; fortified milk and yogurt; and fortified orange juice.

B Vitamins

Going frantic wondering why the apple of your eye is ever so listless and perpetually tired? Vitamin B insufficiency could be playing havoc on his nerves for all you know! B vitamins are a bouquet of eight essential vitamins that play important roles in cell metabolism. These are B_1 (Thiamine), B_2 (Riboflavin), B_3 (Niacin), B_5 (Pantothenic Acid), B_6 (Pyridoxine), B_7 (Biotin), B_9 (Folic Acid) and B_{12} (Cobalamin).

B vitamins have the following functions:
- ❏ They help the body break food down and convert it into energy.
- ❏ They keep nerves and muscle tissue healthy and, thus, help in brain development.
- ❏ They keep the skin and eyes robust.
- ❏ They assist in the formation of haemoglobin in blood cells.
- ❏ They aid with digestion.
- ❏ They help reduce the risk of central nervous system defects in babies.

Vitamin B deficiency could lead to a range of problems including weakness, lack of energy, numbness and light-headedness;

impaired physical and cognitive growth; rapid heartbeat and breathing; pale skin and other dermatological issues; a sore tongue; easy bruising or bleeding in the gums; stomach upset; undesirable weight loss; diarrhoea or constipation; and vitamin B_{12} deficiency anaemia.

Recommended quantity of vitamin B_1 (Thiamine) per day

Birth to 6 months	0.2 mg
Infants 7–12 months	0.3 mg
Children 1–3 years	0.5 mg
Children 4–8 years	0.6 mg
Children 9–13 years	0.9 mg
Teens 14–18 years (boys)	1.2 mg
Teens 14–18 years (girls)	1.0 mg

Recommended quantity of vitamin B_2 (Riboflavin) per day

Birth to 3 years	0.4–0.8 mg
Children 4–6 years	1.1 mg
Children 7–10 years	1.2 mg
Teens 11–18 years (boys)	1.4–1.8 mg
Teens 11–18 years (girls)	1.2–1.3 mg

Recommended quantity of vitamin B_3 (Niacin) per day

Recommended daily allowance of niacin is 2–12 mg per day for children up to eighteen years.

Recommended quantity of vitamin B_5 (Pantothenic Acid) per day

Birth to 3 years	2–3 mg
Children 4–6 years	3–4 mg
Children 7–10 years	4–5 mg
Teens 11–18 years	4–7 mg

Recommended quantity of vitamin B$_6$ (Pyridoxine) per day

Birth to 6 months	0.1 mg
Infants 7–12 months	0.3 mg
Children 1–3 years	0.5 mg
Children 4–8 years	0.6 mg
Children 9–13 years	1.0 mg
Teens 14–18 years (boys)	1.3 mg
Teens 14–18 years (girls)	1.2 mg

Recommended quantity of vitamin B$_7$ (Biotin) per day

Birth to 3 years	10–20 mcg
Children 4–6 years	25 mcg
Children 7–10 years	30 mcg
Children 10–18 years	30–100 mcg

Recommended quantity of vitamin B$_9$ (Folic Acid) per day

Birth to 6 months	65 mcg
Infants 7–12 months	80 mcg
Children 1–3 years	150 mcg
Children 4–8 years	200 mcg
Children 9–13 years	300 mcg
Teens 14–18 years	400 mcg

Recommended quantity of vitamin B$_{12}$ (Cobalamin) per day

Birth to 6 months	0.4 mcg
Infants 7–12 months	0.5 mcg
Children 1–3 years	0.9 mcg
Children 4–8 years	1.2 mcg
Children 9–13 years	1.8 mcg
Teens 14–18 years	2.4 mcg

Good Sources

Good sources of vitamin B include cereals like quinoa, oatmeal, buckwheat, wholewheat, white rice, bulgur and sorghum; beans like soybeans, kidney beans, black-eyed beans, chickpeas and lima beans; seeds like sesame seeds, sunflower seeds and flaxseeds; nuts like almonds, Brazil nuts, cashew nuts, walnuts, peanuts, pistachios and hazelnuts; and peanut butter.

Other sources are fish like mackerel, tuna, salmon, halibut, cod, herring, sardines and trout; fruits like banana, avocado, guava and pomegranate; dried fruits like prunes and dried peaches; lentils; soymilk; dairy products like milk, yogurt, buttermilk, cheese and cottage cheese; vegetables like edamame, mustard greens, turnip greens, potatoes, sweet potato, parsley, peas, beetroot, beet greens, red capsicum, broccoli and asparagus; meats like chicken liver, chicken breast and lamb liver; wheat germ; eggs; and oyster.

Zinc

Zinc plays an important role in ensuring a healthy immune function in kids. It also helps greatly in cell division, cell growth, effective wound healing and the breakdown of carbohydrates. Zinc is also needed for the senses of smell and taste (Alas, what would life be without receptive taste buds?).

A zinc deficiency might cause staggered growth and development in children, delayed wound healing, hair loss, diarrhoea, loss of appetite and undesirable weight loss.

Recommended quantity of zinc per day

Birth to 6 months	2 mg
Infants 7–12 months	3 mg
Children 1–3 years	3 mg
Children 4–8 years	5 mg
Children 9–13 years	8 mg
Teens 14–18 years (boys)	11 mg
Teens 14–18 years (girls)	9 mg

Good Sources

Great sources of zinc include cereals like oatmeal and buckwheat; seeds like sesame seeds, pumpkin seeds, sunflower seeds and flaxseeds; nuts like almonds, Brazil nuts, walnuts, peanuts and pistachios; peanut butter; dried fruits like dried peaches; wheat germ; oysters; lamb liver; and cheese.

Other Minerals

There are a few other minerals that may be needed by the body in very small amounts. These are selenium, iodine, silicon, phosphorous, vitamin K and choline.

The Verdict

The next time your brain goes out of whack trying to unscramble which vitamin or mineral deficiency leads to which malady, don't wrack your brains further—just turn to this chapter and breathe easy!

Chapter 4

Fibre in the Belly

Food that Provides Roughage

My mom's stern and 'no-nonsense look', which distinctly indicated that we had to polish off the 'roughage' served on our plates, is still fresh in my mind. I was baffled by the fuss about the roughage issue back then and scoffed at her fetish for healthy eating, but it all makes sense to me today as a nutritionist, a mother and a discerning adult. Many of you may still be confused about this flurry around fibre and its exact worth in your lives. So, let me deconstruct fibre for you in simple terms.

Main Benefits of Fibre

Fibre or roughage is an essential nutrient that the body needs in big quantities. It helps us in the following body functions:

- It aids in digestion by acting like a sponge and speeding elimination. High-fibre foods add bulk to the bowel and, hence, prevent constipation.
- Eating fibrous foods aids in weight loss as these foods tend to have more volume and fewer calories; they create satiety, staving off hunger pangs for a much longer time.
- Fibre slows the absorption of sugar and keeps glucose levels in check. This helps prevent and manage type 2 diabetes.
- Fibre reduces the risk of heart disease by lowering bad cholesterol and unclogging arteries.

Dietary fibre is only found in plant sources that we consume. This part of the food doesn't get assimilated in the stomach and passes out of the body undigested.

Types of Fibre

Soluble fibre: This dissolves in water and slows down digestion. It is the fibre that keeps us satiated for long and hence, controls unnecessary weight gain. It even helps lower blood cholesterol and glucose levels. Good food sources of soluble fibre are: oats, barley, lentils, legumes (dried peas, kidney beans, lima beans, navy beans, soybeans), apricots, avocados, apples, mangoes, grapefruits, oranges, pears, peaches, plums, ripe banana, strawberries, brussels sprouts, turnip, broccoli, onion, sweet potato, asparagus, cucumber, carrot, celery, peanuts, almond, Brazil nuts, prunes and flaxseeds.

Insoluble fibre: This does not dissolve in water and passes out of the body almost intact without being digested. It adds bulk to food and benefits those who struggle with constipation by promoting the movement of stool through the digestive system. Food sources of insoluble fibre are: whole grains, wholewheat, wheat bran, corn bran, barley, brown rice, lentils, legumes (dried peas, black-eyed peas, kidney beans, lima beans, navy beans), strawberries, kiwifruit, apples, pears, grapes, avocado, zucchini, celery, plantain, cauliflower, broccoli, cabbage, lettuce, onion, Brussels sprouts, asparagus, beetroot, sweet potato, peas, bell peppers, tomato, carrots, cucumber, green beans, dark leafy vegetables, dates, prunes, raisins, almonds, flaxseeds, sunflower seeds and air-popped popcorn.

Soluble and insoluble fibre: Both are found in barley, lentils, legumes (dried peas, kidney beans, lima beans, navy beans), avocados, apples, pears, strawberries, brussels sprouts, broccoli, onion, sweet potato, asparagus, cucumber, carrot, almonds and flaxseeds.

Dietary reference intake for children per day

Ages	Grams per day
Children 1–3 years	19
Children 4–8 years	25
Girls 9–18 years	26
Boys 9–13 years	31
Boys ages 14–18 years	38

The other day, a concerned mother of my ten-year-old client wondered why her son was generally constipated despite being fed a clean, varied diet of fresh homemade meals through the day. A quick gunfire of questions later, I panned out the dilemma of the worried mom. The average daily diet looked like this:

Breakfast: Two eggs (four to five times a week) with white bread and butter/paranthas made of finely ground flour with butter/poori/potato bhaji/noodles without vegetables/ banana pancake with golden syrup/pau-bhaji/aloo tikki burger + milk.

Midday snack: Banana/cheese sandwich with white bread/refined flour mathris/potato wedges/cookies/chicken nuggets/potato smileys.

Lunch: White rice/rotis (made of finely ground flour) + curry/dal.

Evening snack: Banana milkshake/chocolate milkshake.

Snacks on the sly (I had to really coax, bribe and almost plead with the child to dig out this bit): Chocolate bar/cream biscuits/ice cream/potato chips/doughnuts.

Dinner: Rotis (made of finely ground flour) + chicken/mutton/dry subzi (with added potatoes, more often than not).

You will notice that refined flour in preparations, potatoes, banana, meat, eggs, chocolate and milk dominated the diet. These foods are low in fibre and hence, the forerunners in the constipation-inducing department. All the foods in the list are not evil, but they need to be balanced well with fibre-rich foods.

Add around 5 grams of high-fibre foods to your child's diet at each mealtime to ensure the intake of enough fibre through the day.

Best Sources of Fibre

Here is a list of fibre-rich foods that will give your child ample roughage:

Whole grains including oats (cereal, upma, dosa, idli, khichdi); wholewheat flour (roti, bread); barley (roti, salad, soup, khichdi); cracked wheat (salad, khichdi, baked cutlets, cereal); sorghum (salad, khichdi); and buckwheat (roti, khichdi, dhoklas, pancakes).

Fresh fruits including bananas; avocado (dip, guacamole, sandwich spread, soup, salad); guava; Indian gooseberry (mint chutney, mixed vegetable juice); raspberries; pomegranate; pears with skin; apples with skin; kiwi; plums; peaches; and apricots.

Vegetables including peas (cooked or raw); carrots (cooked or raw); broccoli (broth or soup, grilled or sautéed); sweet potato (boiled); turnip greens (cooked); potato with skin (boiled); green beans (cooked); corn (on the cob or boiled or mashed, in popcorn, soup, roti); and spinach.

Legumes and lentils including black-eyed peas (curry, boiled, or three-bean salad); chickpeas (curry, boiled chickpeas salad, chaat or with hummus); kidney beans (curry or three-bean salad); soybeans (sprouts or roasted in snack, nuggets or granules); dried peas (curry or boiled peas salad).

Seeds including flaxseeds (roasted and coarsely powdered, added to roti, cereal, sandwich, smoothie, milkshake, multigrain bread, curries, salads, yogurt); sunflower seeds (roasted and as a snack, trail-mix, multigrain bread or salad); sesame seeds (dip or hummus); pumpkin seeds (roasted and as a snack, trail-mix, multigrain bread or salad).

Nuts including almonds (raw, trail-mix or Indian desserts); walnuts (raw, trail-mix or Indian desserts); pistachios (roasted, trail-mix or Indian desserts); peanuts (roasted, trail-mix, peanut butter, Indian desserts, poha, peanut-jaggery, or energy bar).

Dried fruits including dried figs (raw, trail-mix or Indian desserts); prunes (raw or trail-mix); dates (raw, trail-mix or Indian desserts); dried peaches (raw or trail-mix); dried apricots (raw or trail-mix); raisins (raw, trail-mix or Indian desserts).

No-fibre or Low-fibre Foods

Here is a list of the worst offenders in the fibre department—white bread; refined flour and its preparations; refined pasta and noodles; white rice; meat and fish; poultry; eggs; dairy products including milk, cheese, yogurt, ice cream, cottage cheese and buttermilk; fruit juice; cakes, muffins, doughnuts and refined flour cookies; butter, oil and margarine; chocolate; and sodas.

Smart swaps for increasing fibre in your child's diet

Instead of	Opt for
White bread	Wholewheat bread
Regular pasta	Wholewheat pasta
Plain flour roti	Multigrain roti
White rice	Brown rice
Potato	Sweet potato/potato with skin
French fries/potato wedges/chips	Boiled/baked potatoes with skin
Butter/jam on toast	Peanut butter/avocado paste on toast
Refined flour pizza base/pita bread	Wholewheat pizza base/pita bread
Suji upma	Oats upma
Candies/sweets/chocolates	Dried fruits
Namkeens, biscuits, cakes, pastries, salty snacks	Trail-mix (with nuts, dried fruits and seeds)/chopped raw vegetables with hummus dip/fresh fruit/dried fruits/nuts/boiled corn
Refined flour cakes and muffins	Wholewheat cakes and muffins

Instead of	Opt for
Artificially sweetened and flavoured yogurt	Fresh fruit yogurt
Plain white rice and yellow moong dal khichdi	Brown rice and whole green moong dal khichdi with vegetables
Salad with creamy dressings	Plain and fresh vegetable salad/boiled chickpeas salad/sprouts salad/with herbs/guacamole
Fruit juice	Whole fruit
Chocos/Froot loops in milk	Oats in milk with chopped fresh fruit and/or dried fruits and nuts

A caveat: If it's a high-fibre meal that your child is enjoying, do not forget to team it up with an adequate amount of water. A high-fibre diet will only aid in digestion and cure constipation if it is accompanied with enough fluids. On the flipside, a very high-fibre meal without enough fluids could cause abdominal discomfort and dehydration.

The Verdict

Keep offering a variety of fibrous foods to your children to make them a part of their balanced diet. While the kids get into the habit of eating healthy fibrous foods, you'll set the tone for a lifetime of healthy eating. So, clear out your kitchen cabinets of all chips, cookies and soda and train your child to nibble on fibre-rich foods instead.

Chapter 5

Nutrient-infused, Immunity-boosting Heroes

Vegetables and Fruits

Offer most children vegetables and fruits and chances are you'll come up against a gigantic mental block. During our childhood, our parents insisted that we polish off our plates stacked with veggies and chow down the evening fruit without a whimper regardless of whether we liked or loathed them. In this day and age, almost the entire planet seems to be shouting from the rooftops about the virtues of fruits and vegetables. The Internet is abuzz about the benefits of these 'nature's goodies' (and not without reason). So, what is it about these brightly hued, scrumptious and much-touted edibles that makes them indispensable?

Benefits of Consuming Fruits and Vegetables

The dossier on all-natural fruits and vegetables proclaims that they're cardinal to a child's health. Here's how:

A Powerhouse of Nutrients

It should come as no surprise that fruits and vegetables are crammed with several macronutrients, micronutrients and other essential nutrients such as vitamins, minerals, fibre and antioxidants. They're packed with vitamins A, C, E, K and folate. These vitamins are responsible for sharp vision, healthy skin, healthy teeth and bones, a strong immune system and cell growth. Folate helps the body form red blood cells. Fruits and vegetables are living quarters for various minerals like calcium, iron, magnesium, potassium, zinc and selenium. While calcium helps strengthen bones and teeth; iron is critical for making haemoglobin, magnesium has a role in almost 300 crucial bodily functions, potassium regulates fluid balance in the blood and zinc helps in building immunity and is needed for the senses of smell and taste. Fibre speeds up elimination, preventing constipation. It also reduces bad cholesterol and lowers the risk of heart disease.

Filling Yet Not Fattening

Are you conscious of your young one's weight and looking for low-calorie-but-nutritious-foods? Voila! Look no further— vegetables and fruits it is! These foods are much lower in calories compared to extensively consumed foods like heavy curries, pasta, pizzas, burgers, patties, fried snacks and cheesy foods. Fruits and vegetables are crammed with macronutrients, micronutrients, water and fibre and yet they're very low in calories with negligible fat. They create satiety due to their water and roughage content. Children can rarely overeat these hearty goodies.

Reduces the Risk of Diseases

Eating lots of fruits and vegetables reduces the risk of ailments such as heart disease, type 2 diabetes, obesity, intestinal illnesses, kidney stones and certain types of cancers. Daily consumption of these foods also keeps blood pressure in control, helps nervous health and arrests bone loss.

Essential for Brain Development

It's scientifically proven that a diet deficient in complex carbohydrates can affect a child's cognitive health. Fruits are a great source of energy for young minds, while vegetables are home to many brain-friendly nutrients such as lycopene, beta-carotene, iron, vitamins A, B_9 (folic acid), C, E and K and dietary fibre. Complex and fibrous carbohydrates regulate the brain glucose levels, boost mental alertness, lower stress levels and sharpen mental acuity.

Essential for Physical Performance

Carbohydrates are the main source of energy for the body. Young athletes and active physically children expend more energy than others and, therefore, need more carbohydrates. Most fruits are good sources of energy. Banana stands out amongst fruits as the chief energy-fixer. Some vegetables that can replenish depleted energy are potatoes, sweet potatoes, beetroot, carrots, beans and peas, as these are rich sources of complex carbohydrates. Other than carbohydrates, children also need some other nutrients for enhancing physical performance such as calcium, iron, magnesium, zinc and vitamins B, C and D. Fruits and vegetables that are good sources of these nutrients are:

Vegetables: All green leafy vegetables, root vegetables, broccoli, beetroot, carrot, peas, cabbage, capsicum, squash, tomatoes, cauliflower, green beans and pumpkin.

Fruits: Orange, lemon, banana, plums, pomegranate, papaya, guava, kiwi, cantaloupe, honeydew melon, mango, watermelon, strawberries, raspberries, pineapple, apricot, Indian gooseberry and avocado.

Builds Immunity

A strong immune system is crucial for children to keep illnesses at bay so that they are able to study and play regularly. Nutrients such as vitamins A, C and E; minerals like zinc and selenium; and omega-3 and omega-6 fatty acids build the body's resistance to infections by fighting off free radicals and enhancing the functioning of white blood cells. Fruits and vegetables rich in the following nutrients:

Fruits: Orange, lemon, banana, plum, muskmelon, mango, apricot, pomegranate, grapefruit, tangerine, papaya, pineapple, watermelon, guava, sweet lime, kiwifruit, strawberries, raspberries, cherries, Indian gooseberry and jamun;

Vegetables: Capsicums (red, green), broccoli, cauliflower, cabbage (green, red), carrot, sweet potato, white potato, pumpkin, butternut squash, spinach, peas, asparagus, beetroot greens, mustard greens, turnip greens, tomato, bok choy, parsley, brussels sprouts, green beans and onion.

Colour Me Bright

Interestingly, the colours of fruits and vegetables speak volumes about their nutritious value, as different colours connote the presence of specific nutrients in each of these vibrantly hued foods. It is advisable to offer a little of each colour for packing a nutritional punch to your child's health. There are five colour categories:

Red: Red fruits and vegetables get their colour from two antioxidants: lycopene and anthocyanin. These antioxidants reduce the risk of cardiovascular disease, certain cancers and macular degeneration of the eyes. The red fruits and vegetables are: tomatoes, strawberries, raspberries, cherries, cranberries, watermelon, pink grapefruit, red apples, red guavas, red cabbage, red pepper, red radish and beetroot.

Orange and yellow: Orange and yellow fruits and vegetables get their colour from the natural carotenoid pigment called cryptoxanthin. Our body converts this into vitamin A, a nutrient that is needed for healthy eyes, teeth, bones and skin. The best sources of carotenoids are cantaloupe, lemon, orange, mango, papaya, pineapple, apricots, peaches, carrots, sweet potato, sweet corn, yellow bell pepper, winter squash and pumpkin.

Blue and purple: Plant pigments called anthocyanins, which are antioxidants, hand down blue and purple colours to various fruits and vegetables. Anthocyanins help reduce the risk of cardiovascular disease and most cancers. The best sources of anthocyanins are plums, purple grapes, purple cabbage and eggplants.

White: There are certain pigments and antioxidant-rich flavonoids such as quercetin, anthoxanthin and allicin that give white and yellowish white vegetables their colour. The consumption of foods with these antioxidants help in protecting against bad cholesterol and lower the risk of heart disease. They even help to reduce the possibility of certain types of cancers in adulthood. Some vital white foods are: apples, pears, bananas, cauliflower, cucumbers, garlic, onions, mushrooms, shallots and turnips.

Green: Naturally occurring carotenoids called lutein and zeaxanthin render the green colour to fruits and vegetables. A phytochemical called sulforaphane is also present in cruciferous vegetables. Green vegetables are especially very healthy as they're rich sources of calcium, iron, potassium, magnesium and vitamins A, B_9 (folic acid), C, E and K. Green vegetables include both dark green leafy vegetables and cruciferous vegetables. Since green vegetables are the hub of this cluster of crucial minerals and vitamins, regular consumption will lead to several health benefits. They are beneficial for bones, teeth and eyes. The greens with vitamin K help in blood clotting too. Cruciferous vegetables are known for their cancer-fighting property. Some green vegetables are: asparagus, broccoli, brussels sprouts, bok choy, celery, cucumbers, green beans, cabbage, shallots, green bell peppers, mustard greens, spinach, beet greens, methi leaves, lettuce, okra, peas, watercress, zucchini, bottle gourd and bitter gourd. Some green fruits are green apples, grapes, pears, kiwifruit, avocado and honeydew melon.

How Much Is Enough?

Although the amount of fruits and vegetables to be consumed by children depends upon age, gender, body size and their physical activity levels. The advice from the World Health Organization is that children should eat five portions a day of fruits and vegetables in total. Each portion should be around 80 grams so that children get a minimum of 400 grams of these super-healthy foods daily. (For age-wise and gender-wise quantity recommendations, check out the complete 'Calorie Grids' table).

As an approximate guide, a single portion is the amount of food that can fit into the palm of your hand.

Quick Fix for Veggie-loathers

We may talk about the numerous benefits of this colourful group of foods, but let's face the fact that there are as many children who belong to the 'I hate veggies' club as the veggie-lovers. If your little one gags on ingesting vegetables and spurns them, don't be crestfallen and DON'T GIVE UP! Hold onto your resolve and try the following tips till the apple of your eye relents:

- ❏ Change the way you cook vegetables. Even if you change one element in a vegetable dish, it could transform the way your child perceives it.
- ❏ Change the cooking method or cuisine. If you cook a dish in Indian style, try cooking it in the Continental or Mexican or some other style.
- ❏ Experiment with one or more ingredients like herbs and spices used for that dish.
- ❏ Change or add a sauce or a dip or a salad dressing to give the dish a zing.
- ❏ Camouflage and add vegetables to as many dishes as possible. For instance:

- Add chopped or diced vegetables to lasagne, stews, gravies, soups, salads, sandwiches, omelettes, uttapam or idlis.
- Add pureed vegetables like spinach to smoothies/curries/roti/idlis.
- Add vegetable tidbits to pies, casserole dishes, quiches, pizza or pasta.
- Add leftover vegetable dishes or subzi to make stuffed roti or parantha
- Prepare a platter of assorted foods and arrange it attractively. It should ideally look colourful with the main dish, side dish, a healthy dip and grilled vegetables on the side such as zucchini, baby corn, green beans, carrot and broccoli.
- Serve vegetables raw with a healthy dip to children who have an aversion to cooked vegetables. They may love the raw, mild taste and may surprise you by lapping up their share of vegetables.
- Offer mixed vegetable juice to your child—a delicious way of consuming vegetables. Carrot, beetroot, tomato and cilantro and mint leaves taste great in liquid form. To make it more nutritious and tastier, add a slice or two of orange, an Indian gooseberry and a dash of lemon juice to it.

The Verdict

There is a wide gamut of fruits and vegetables with varied nutritional profiles available in vibrant and alluring colours. Unlike most other food types, fruits and vegetables are naturally low in fat, cholesterol, sodium and calories. In short, they're the foundation of a healthy diet. Therefore, it's prudent to offer varied coloured fruits and vegetables to your children every day.

Chapter 6
That Divine Cooler
Water

The historian, Thomas Fuller had said, 'We never know the worth of water till the well is dry.' The quote can aptly be modified in the current context to say, 'We never know the worth of water till our body runs dry.' It's no secret that water is essential for life. It is a vital nutrient for the body as 60–80 per cent of the body weight is water. A human being can survive without food for over a month but only for a maximum of two to three days without water.

Despite being clued in on the importance of water for our body, we still overlook its significance. Most of us have a low water intake and drink it only when we're thirsty. This is a sign that we have already reached the dehydration mark and are only trying to balance out the water that our body would have lost. We seldom forget to sip our morning tea or the evening cuppa which we treat as a sacrosanct ritual, but conveniently forget to tank up on the lifesaving fluid called water. A third of my clients consume an inadequate amount of water, ranging from two to eight glasses a day. The average is around four glasses a day.

It is even more important for children to be well hydrated. Mental performance comes down substantially when one is thirsty. Kids also exercise substantially more than adults, their bodies are much less heat-tolerant and they're more susceptible to getting dehydrated. The above reasons make it imperative for children to follow a strict daily hydration regime. Since we don't pay due homage to this celestial beverage, we obviously fail to teach our children to value the same.

It is almost customary for me to rattle out the importance of water to each one of my clients. So, here I reel off on its virtues again, yakking about the importance of good hydration.

The Importance of Water

Water plays a crucial role in ensuring that your child's body functions efficiently by helping him stay healthy. Here's how:

- ❏ It ensures that the body functions normally and the child is not dehydrated.
- ❏ It flushes out toxins that can lead to illnesses.
- ❏ It helps transport nutrients efficiently to the blood and various internal organs.
- ❏ It helps in digestion and keeps constipation at bay.
- ❏ It reduces the risk of urinary tract infections.
- ❏ It helps keep the body cool by maintaining the body's internal water balance and regulating body temperature.
- ❏ Its regular intake helps in maintaining a healthy weight, bringing down the risk of childhood obesity.
- ❏ Sufficient hydration is believed to improve children's mental performance and cognitive skills.
- ❏ It aids in the physical fitness of children by keeping their energy from burning out.
- ❏ It regenerates all the living cells.

Symptoms of Dehydration

When a child doesn't drink enough water, he could be mildly dehydrated, which is the least of the damage possible. Some of the more alarming effects of dehydration include fatigue, headaches, light-headedness or dizziness, constipation, a dry mouth or dry skin, muscle weakness, drowsiness and exhaustion, decreased urine output or dark yellow and smelly urine, diminished concentration and difficulty thinking clearly.

Remember that your child needs to drink even more water

in hot and sultry weather and during strenuous physical activity. So, don't wait for your child's thirst to come a-calling; offer him the life-saver aqua even before he shows signs of being thirsty.

Dehydration and Exercise

I remember a disconcerting anecdote recounted to me by a distressed parent of a sixteen year old. A very athletic and a fit guy he may have been, but he managed to scare the living daylights out of his parents one day. It was when he collapsed and passed out after a ninety-minute fitness session. Although he regained consciousness within a few seconds, it spooked his folks badly, leaving them distraught for a few days. The jolt was stronger since the parents were habitually circumspect about his food habits in conformance with his dietary needs as an athlete and therefore, could not gauge where they could have slackened. What followed was a flurry of medical tests including the ominous and unsettling CT scan. While fortunately, all the medical reports came out clean, the circumstantial evidence during the post-tests medical consultation pointed towards dehydration being the sole culprit for the blackout.

Inadequate hydration can cause muscle fatigue, leading to reduced brain and body coordination. This can cause light-headedness followed by a fainting spell. In more severe cases, dehydration could impair the body's ability to cool itself down through perspiration. This, in turn, could lead to a life-threatening condition called heat stroke. In the case of the teen, the boy was often exercising for extended periods without drinking much water.

Children can't be held completely responsible in such cases. Kids being kids, they can often be so immersed in their activities that they may not even realize that they're thirsty and need to pause to refill their water tanks. We as parents need to instil this habit in them, as habits get established very early in childhood.

Dehydration and Cognitive Performance

Dehydration can act as a killjoy for your child's mental performance and cognitive abilities. Water makes up almost 80 per cent of the brain and children need to think clearly to be able to tackle academic pressure well. In the absence of sufficient fluids in the body, a child can experience irritability, blurred memory and lack of concentration, affecting his/her academic performance.

How Much Is Enough?

The amount of water or other water-based fluids that a child needs depends on many factors such as age, gender, metabolism, physical activity, environment and weather. However, there is a minimum recommendation of drinking water for kids too.

The approximate recommended daily amount of fluids is:

1–3 years: 5 cups (1 litre)
4–8 years: 6–7 cups (1.3 litres)
9–13 years: 8–10 cups (1.6–2.4 litres)
14 years and above: 10–13cups (2.5–3 litres or more)

Other Fluid Sources that Hydrate

Although water is the best drink to quench your little one's thirst, there are other fluids and foods with high water content that serve well to hydrate the little bodies. These include juices (dilute and offer only occasionally due to their high sugar content); coconut water; fresh lemonade; milk and milk products like yogurt and buttermilk; foods like fruits, vegetables and soups; and sports drinks.

Water Versus Other Sweetened Drinks

Don't soft drinks and sports drinks have enough water? Yes, they do! But remember, they are loaded with empty calories in the form of sugar. That's a package deal! Regular consumption of these sugar-laden beverages can lead to excessive weight gain, diabetes and tooth decay. Although, fresh fruit juices are naturally sweetened drinks, excessive consumption too can lead to the same problems. So, if you have to offer fresh fruit juices/sports drinks to your child because he/she is underweight, it is wise to water it down to dilute the sugar.

It's best to hydrate your child with plain water since it does as good a job as sugar-laden sports drinks. Water has no calories unlike juices and other sweetened drinks, so it hydrates without the negative impact of extra calories.

Pointers to Prevent Dehydration

Normally, all of us lose some body water every single day through sweat, urine, stool, tears, or even during ailments like fever, vomiting and diarrhoea. While this fluid loss gets replaced through the water in the food, the water that we lose through intense activity or the hot and sultry weather needs to be replaced through the intake of regular water or other water-based fluids. Here are a few tips to keep the lid tightly on dehydration:

- ❏ Always pack a water bottle along when your child is going to school or for a day trip.
- ❏ Offer your child water every hour or so during hot weather. She may not drink much every time you offer her water, but even a few sips will go a long way in ensuring that she is well hydrated through the day.
- ❏ Offer an extra water bottle to your child if he is going to play an outdoor sport or any other physical activity. Insist that he drinks water before the start of the activity, during the activity at regular intervals and afterwards to replenish the fluids lost through sweat.
- ❏ Offer plenty of water and other healthy fluids to kids when they're sick, especially during fever, vomiting and diarrhoea.

❏ In hot and humid weather, put a frozen ice pop maker in your child's water bottle to help her quench her thirst effectively.

❏ It should be the responsibility of the teachers/guardians/caretakers to offer water or other hydrating fluids to younger kids on a regular basis while these kids are in day care.

❏ If plain water is boring and humdrum for your child, make the water-drinking ritual a tad bit exciting by adding fun flavours to it such as a dash of lemon juice, orange slices, watermelon cubes, freshly cut cucumbers, or a sprig of mint.

❏ A lesson pertaining to the importance of hydration should be incorporated in younger kids' syllabus. This would help greatly in making them aware about the significance of water early in life. The lessons taught in school by the teachers are taken as gospel truth by most children and are most likely to be followed through their growing-up years.

❏ Drink water regularly in the presence of your child so that they mimic you till it becomes a habit with them. Leading by example is an effective way of getting your kids to do what you want them to.

The Verdict

By now, it should be crystal clear to all you parents that you can't rely on your children to come up to you every time and say, 'Mom/Dad, give me water. I am really thirsty.' Just like you plan your child's food each day, drinking water should also be a part of your child's planned daily diet. So, go get them drunk on the finest beverage up for grabs. It won't hurt your pocket and won't give them the dreaded hangover. Can it get any better?

Chapter 7
The Dreaded Trinity
Sugar–Salt–Fat

'Sugar–salt–fat' is the three-fanged monster that seduces human taste buds and takes them for a ride. The ride can turn disastrous when it dislodges the merry-maker from her healthy seat and hurls her into the dark pit of lifestyle diseases. In the garb of enhancing the savouriness of the food, this deadly trio gets people hooked on to them. Children are even more vulnerable to getting lured by this addiction as they are of an impressionable age and get driven by the call of their tender taste buds.

Unfortunately, most of the food available outside the house is either laden with enormous fat, excessive salt, dollops of sugar or in worst cases, all three. Fatty foods, sugar-laden treats and excessively salty snacks no doubt make the food more appealing, but they also easily pile up a humongous amount of calories. Most foods with a generous amount of these three evils have empty calories with few or no nutrients at all.

Let's carry out an exposé on the worrisome threesome and get to the bottom of the complete truth, emerging wiser at the end of the unmasking.

Sweet Nothings: Sugar

Sugar is not an all-black evil. Young bodies need carbohydrates for energy and sugar is the primary source of carbohydrates that impart quick energy. The problem occurs in the wrong selection of the source of sugar or when too much sugar of any type is consumed too often. Excess sugar in the body can eventually be stored as body fat in the liver and muscles, leading to the risk of obesity, type 2 diabetes and heart diseases.

There are two types of sugars contained in food and drinks: 1) Natural sugars—these naturally occur in many foods like fruit (fructose), dairy products (lactose) and honey. 2) Added sugars—those that are artificially added to foods, such as sucrose, maltose, corn syrup and maple syrup. These are found in confectionery, sweets and soft drinks. Let's clear away all the haze around these to recognize them for what they are.

Natural Sugars

The three natural sugar types are: fructose, sucrose and galactose. While harm occurs due to excess sugar in the body, not all natural sugar is evil. Therefore, their food sources are divided into two categories: the healthy and the harmful.

The Healthy Sources: These foods have low glycemic indices, which means that their consumption leads to a slower absorption of glucose into the blood that does not create constant spikes in blood glucose level. Some food items are not only good sources of energy but also of other nutrients such as vitamins, minerals, proteins and dietary fibre. These include fruits like grapes, pear, apple, banana, plum, orange, pineapple, berries, kiwi, papaya, muskmelon and peach; vegetables like red capsicum, onion, sweet corn, sugarcane, sweet potato, carrot, beetroot, celery, broccoli and mushrooms; whole grains like wheat, maize, sago, rice and soy flour; dried fruits like raisins, prunes, dried apricots and dried figs; dairy products like milk and yogurt; dried beans like kidney beans, chickpeas and black-eyed peas; and honey (in restricted quantities).

All these foods items may be simple sugar sources, but they're packed with nutrients such as protein, vitamins, minerals, fibre and phytochemicals. While fruits, milk products and root vegetables should be consumed by children regularly, dried fruits should be eaten in moderation in case the child is overweight. Honey boasts of some beneficial enzymes and nutrients as compared to empty calories of sugar. However, parents should observe moderation even in offering honey to their kids as too much sugar, even in its natural form on a regular basis, can cause insulin-resistance, leading to diabetes in adulthood.

The Harmful Sources: These foods have high glycemic indices, which indicates that their consumption leads to a speedy absorption of glucose into the blood that eventually causes steep blood glucose spikes. These food items include table sugar; corn syrup; corn starch; tapioca syrup; maple sugar; fruit juices (often); molasses; agave nectar; table sugar (white); caramel; and invert syrup

Consumption of the above sugar sources leads to unhealthy cravings for more sugary foods and can lead to further bingeing on sweet foods even without hunger. This can form a habit difficult to break and can lead to lifestyle illnesses like obesity, diabetes and heart ailments in adulthood.

Added Sugars

Added sugars also known as 'non-nutritive sweeteners', are those that are added to foods or beverages when they are processed, prepared, or added at the table to make the food taste more appetizing. These add calories that are bereft of any nutrients or fibre. This type of sugar is bad sugar as it increases your child's risk of piling on undesirable weight, developing type 2 diabetes and heart disease just the way harmful simple sugar sources impact young bodies. This is the category we really need to worry about. The problem is that the 'sweet taste' is most developed in children, therefore, their taste buds cry out for foods like chocolates, cakes, ice cream and candies. The list of these foods is, unfortunately, very long and ever-growing. I have tried to list as many as possible to give a fair idea of the sweet devils that lure our children.

Items with added sugars include beverages like soft drinks, energy drinks, canned fruit juices, fresh fruit juices and sports drinks; confectionery items like cakes, doughnuts, pastries and cookies; candies and chewing gums; chocolates; ice cream; sweetened milkshakes; tinned fruits in syrup; granola bars, energy bars and protein bars; dried fruits with added sugar syrup; desserts like fruit cream and custard; Indian desserts like halwa, kheer, laddoos and shahi tukda; sauces or spreads like coleslaw, barbecue sauce, ketchup, commercially made peanut butter, chocolate sauce and chocolate spreads; flavoured fruit yogurt; sweetened cereals like muesli, chocolate flakes and fruit loops; and processed foods.

Drawbacks of Feasting on the Sweet Devils

Let me echo my concern yet again by stating that sugar is as addictive as illicit drugs like weed and hash, as it impacts the same feel-good chemical compounds, serotonin and dopamine. So, help your children steer clear of the temptation of overindulging in it or else they may be at a risk of suffering from a range of ailments including type 2 diabetes, obesity, coronary heart diseases, mood swings, hyperactivity and tooth decay.

All in the Family: Sugar and Its Numerous Nicknames

Don't get duped by the infinite fancy names that you read on the food labels. Sugar sells through many aliases. Always read the ingredient labels on processed foods carefully to identify added sugars masked in glitzy names such as table sugar, honey, brown sugar, raw sugar (turbinado sugar), sucrose, dextrose, fructose, lactose, glucose, maltose, corn syrup, high fructose corn syrup, corn syrup solids, fruit juice concentrate, invert syrup, malt syrup, maple syrup, molasses, nectars (peach/pear), white granulated sugar, anhydrous dextrose, demerara sugar, milled sugar, confectioner's sugar, treacle, rice syrup, xylose, cane crystals, evaporated cane juice, cane sugar/syrup (golden syrup), barley malt, crystalline fructose, beet sugar, date sugar and coconut sugar.

Sugary Foods Masquerading as 'Health Foods'

Sugar with its wily ways can sneak in stealthily into your body through many of these so-called health foods. While we may be sitting smugly thinking that we're feeding our kids 'health foods' (thanks to the 'low-fat' labels on containers), sweet calories may be sitting pretty in these foods in the garb of taste-enhancers. Therefore, some of these so-called 'low-fat' foods could be much higher in calories than the normal 'non-low-fat' health foods. So, be discerning while buying these 'health foods'; read the labels carefully to scout for fats, sugar and sodium with their numerous alternate names.

Some examples of these 'health foods' high on the calorie count are canned fruit juices or fresh fruit juices; breakfast cereals with fruit loops, honey loops, frosted wheat bits, raisin bran crunches, banana nut crunches or oatmeal crisp crunches; cereal, granola or protein bars; dried fruits coated with sugar syrup like dried cherries or dried cranberries; nuts with sugar coating; a ready-made trail-mix with choco-chips, sweetened coconut flakes and glazed fruit bits; ready-made creamy peanut butter made with sugar or honey; sauces, dips, dressings and spreads like chilli salsa, honey mustard; low-fat diet foods like namkeens with added sugar; fruit milkshakes with added sugar; and packaged curd, fruit yogurt or sweetened probiotic drinks.

Maximum Daily Allowance

The American Heart Association recommends the following allowance for sugar:

- ❐ Preschoolers: Not more than about 16.7 grams per day.
- ❐ Ages 4–8 years: Not more than about 12.5 grams per day.
- ❐ Pre-teens and teenagers: Between 21 and 33 grams per day.

Some Approaches to Cut Down Sugar Menace in Your Child's Life

Offer homemade desserts: Instead of relenting to requests for commercial puddings and ice creams, make fresh fruit/dried fruit puddings at home, such as fruit yogurt, fruit custard and lightly sweetened rice kheer. These will serve the dual purpose of satiating the craving for sweets as well as getting the daily quota of fruits into the system. Use the sweetness of fruits or minimal honey to make these puddings.

Opt for healthier foods to gratify sweet cravings: Instead of heavy milkshakes which are loaded with milk fat and sugar, make low-calorie fruit smoothies with skimmed milk (without/with minimal honey) or milkshakes with skimmed milk and just fruit (without added sugar).

Avoid pre-sweetened cereals: Go in for low-calorie but healthy cereals such as oatmeal, broken wheat (daliya), natural muesli, multigrain puffs instead of sugary choco bits and fruity loops. For sweetness, add chopped fresh fruit, dried fruits, or a little honey.

Boot out the juice: Serve fruit instead of fruit juice to cut down sugar calories, as fruit also adds fibre that is needed for digestive health.

Pack clean: Do not pack cookies, candies, cakes, chocolates and other sweets in your kids' tiffin boxes. They are likely to fill their little tummies with this junk and avoid the healthier part of the tiffin.

Avoid sweet rewards: Granting candies and desserts as rewards for good behaviour sends the wrong message to children that desserts are definitely better than other foods. Children then form a habit of demanding sugary treats in return for good conduct and get hooked on to these sweet treats. Rewards should be in other forms, like extra time in the park or a movie outing.

Remember, it is perfectly fine when your kids indulge in sweet treats occasionally, but don't let these added sugars upset the apple cart (read, good health) of your child through regular consumption. Try to add natural sugars in her diet through whole grains, fruits, vegetables, low-fat milk and milk products, dried fruits, dried beans, nuts and root vegetables. Adding a little sweetness to your child's palate is definitely not a crime, but moderation is the key.

The Fat Sheet (Fats)

As discussed in the earlier chapter on macronutrients, fats are critical for both, the physical and mental growth of children. Young kids, in particular, need enough of them in their diet to help the brain and nervous system develop normally.

Good Fats

Just as a recap, let's revisit the benefits of good fats for children. Good fats supply fuel for the body; help it to absorb vital fat-soluble vitamins such as A, D, E and K; and generate efficient growth hormones. They are also beneficial to the heart as they reduce bad cholesterol. They are needed for healthy cell membranes and are essential for brain development. Furthermore, good fats insulate all nervous system tissues in the body and cushion the vital organs. In addition, they control belly fat as they help kids feel full for a longer duration, preventing them from bingeing

Good fats can be found in fatty fish like salmon, tuna, mackerel, catfish, herring, anchovies and trout; oils such as olive, canola, soybean, corn, peanut, flaxseed, sesame, almond, sunflower and safflower; nuts like hazelnuts, almonds, walnuts, pistachios, Brazil nuts, cashews and pine nuts; seeds like flaxseeds, sesame and pumpkin; olives; peanut butter; and avocados.

Having eulogized the 'good' fats, it's time to move to the 'bad' and the 'ugly' ones. Remember, a gram of fat has more than twice the calories than a gram of carbohydrates or protein. So, 1 gram of fat provides nine calories, whereas 1 gram of carbs or protein provides four calories.

The Fatty Evils

We know the cliché well by now that *all fats are not made equal*. While good fats in controlled quantities are beneficial for the body, there are two main types of potentially harmful fats, namely saturated and trans fat.

Saturated fats are solid at room temperature. They emanate from animal sources of food, such as red meat, poultry and full-fat dairy products. The dietary recommendation for this fat is no more than 7 per cent per day.

Trans fat, also known as hydrogenated fat, is mostly made from oils through a food processing method called partial hydrogenation.

Both saturated fat and trans fat can be catastrophic for our children (detailed list in the chapter on macronutrients). It's really sad to witness ever-increasing cases of juvenile obesity, type 2 diabetes, dyspepsia, hypertension, high LDL cholesterol, low HDL cholesterol, clogged arteries and other heart ailments. These are the bad fats found in the food of most restaurants, processed foods and packaged foods such as French fries, cakes, cookies, pastries, chocolates, pizzas, burgers, doughnuts, namkeens, creamy cheese, mayonnaise, ice cream, coconut chips, potato wafers, full-fat milkshakes—the list goes on.

No doubt, fats do enhance the flavour of food, but they also make people crave for them, turning many of our little ones into junk food addicts. It's very easy to overindulge in them as they're present in almost every food that children love.

The sources of these 'fatty evils' are full fat dairy products like full-fat milk, butter, cream, cheese, high-fat cottage cheese (paneer), full-fat curd and clarified butter (ghee); animal products such as liver, other organ meats, poultry, sausages, salamis and bacon; desserts like fruit cream, kheer, halwa, sweetmeats (mithai), ice cream and ice cream shakes; heavy milkshakes; hydrogenated oils, palm oil and coconut oil; margarine, shortenings and lard; salad dressings and sandwich spreads such as Caesar salad dressing, ranch dressing, thousand island dressing, mayonnaise and coleslaw; coconut products; egg yolks; most commercially prepared food items such as burgers, pizzas, hotdogs, cakes, doughnuts, chips and cookies; and all deep-fried food items.

There are, in addition, high-fat foods masquerading as 'health foods'. These include full-fat dairy products like milk, yogurt and cottage cheese (paneer); creamy cheese in the form of spreads; and red meat. This list would also include readymade dips or dressings like hummus dip and tahini loaded with olive oil, hung curd dip made from full fat milk, ranch dressing, Italian dressing and thousand island dressing. Some salads loaded with fatty dressings and croutons like Caesar salad, Waldorf salad and Russian salad should be avoided or consumed in moderation. The same holds true for full-fat milkshakes; commercially made popcorn with butter; chicken or fish gravies with lots of oil or butter; chicken or fish tikkas and kebabs with loads of butter basting; and chicken with skin.

Maximum Daily Allowance

The National Institute of Health, USA, recommends the following dietary fat calories per day for children:

❑ Preschoolers: 30–40 per cent of total calories per day.
❑ Ages 4–18: 25–35 per cent of total calories per day.

Remember, calories from saturated fats should not exceed 10 per cent of total fat calories per day. Also, reduce the intake of solid fats as much as possible for the health of your child's heart. So, while low-fat diets are not meant for children, a diet high in fats can also be counterproductive to their overall health.

Some Pointers to Cut Down Bad Fats from Your Child's Diet

Avoid processed/ready-to-eat meats: These include sausages, frankfurters, salami and ham. Buy fresh and skinless meat and fish instead.

Say no to full-fat dairy products: Buy dairy products that are only low-fat or skimmed. Kids above three years of age do not need full-fat dairy products unless they're seriously underweight or malnourished.

Avoid fried meat: It packs in a humongous amount of calories from saturated fat. Instead, go for baked, broiled, grilled or roasted fish and chicken without skin to get an adequate dosage of good fats.

Go light on dips and dressings: Try lighter low-fat dips or dressing options. A lot of these are delicious as you could experiment with a lot of healthier ingredients such as vinegar, mustard, lemon juice, hung curd and herbs.

Go for oil swaps: Avoid solid oils for cooking. Instead, opt for cooking oils high in omega-3 and omega-6 like olive and canola.

Cut saturated fat: Try replacing butter, margarine, hydrogenated oils, double cream and fresh cream with unsaturated oils (like canola and olive) and leaner sandwich spreads (hung curd, mint chutney, hummus or guacamole).

Pick MUFA/PUFA: Opt for foods rich in monounsaturated fats (MUFAs) and polyunsaturated fats (PUFAs). For instance, swap red meat or deli meats with oily fish at least twice a week.

Don't go overboard with fat: Since all fats, good as well as bad, are very high in calories, avoid overkill (even of PUFA- and MUFA-rich foods). There are nine calories in a gram of fat as compared to four calories in a gram of protein and carbohydrates each.

Beware of reduced-fat and low-fat claims: Before buying food, check the label for hidden fats. Avoid foods with the following entries on the food label: partially hydrogenated; saturated fats; trans fats; solid fats; meats with skin; and/or cholesterol

Pinch Off Salt

While the world shouts from the rooftop vilifying the two villains—sugar and fat—salt manages to slither away, its maliciousness getting little notice.

Benefits of Just that Pinch of Salt

Too much salt is bad, yet it would be unfair if I make it out to be an all-wicked villain with no virtue, so here are the reasons why your kitchen should not be made salt-free!

Salt helps the body to maintain electrolyte balance. It regulates body fluid and blood pressure. It enables the proper functioning of the nervous system as it helps transmit messages through the entire body and also supports the proper contraction and relaxation of muscles. Salt also helps in digestion.

Drawbacks of Rattling that Salt Shaker Too Much, Too Often

Now that we have extolled the virtues of that pinch of salt, let us now delve into the darker side of overconsumption of salt. Too much salt can cause hypertension, increase the risk of heart disease and in extreme cases, lead to heart failure. It can cause renal disease as kidneys can't keep up with the sodium build-up. In the worst cases, it could lead to coma due to the elevated level of sodium in blood.

Moreover, salt can lead to fluid retention, which can bloat up a person significantly.

Popular Sodium Offenders in the Market with Approximate Sodium Content

About 80 per cent of salt that children who enjoy fast foods consume, comes from frozen, processed or packaged food and restaurant meals. 'A typical fast-food meal can contain up to 5,000 mg of sodium—more than double the daily recommended limit,' says Edward J. Roccella, PhD, of the National Heart, Lung and Blood Institute, Maryland, USA.

It's not just table salt that can send your blood pressure shooting through the roof—it may come as a jolt to see sodium flood the body through some innocuous-looking favourites. Take a look at some of them:

- ❒ Table salt, baking soda, baking powder (10 grams): 3,800 mg
- ❒ Potato/tortilla chips (100 grams): 524–856 mg
- ❒ Nuts, salted (peanuts, almonds, cashews) (50 grams): 1,200 mg
- ❒ Breakfast cereal, dry, all varieties (1 cup): 200–250 mg
- ❒ Bacon, cooked (50 grams): 1,000–1,300 mg
- ❒ Salami or pepperoni, all varieties (50 grams): 500–1,100 mg
- ❒ Sausage, all varieties, cooked (50 grams): 280–600 mg
- ❒ Chicken nuggets, cooked (50 grams): 220–280 mg
- ❒ Processed cheese slices (50 grams): 685–794 mg
- ❒ Cream cheese (1 tbsp): 43 mg
- ❒ Popcorn (100 grams): 1,500 mg
- ❒ Instant packaged soup (100 ml): 840 mg
- ❒ Sauces and spreads (100 grams): 1,200 mg
- ❒ White bread (1 slice): 170–238 mg
- ❒ Pizza (1 slice): 440–774 mg
- ❒ Creamed style corn (1 cup): 730 mg
- ❒ Cucumber, pickled (1 piece): 833 mg
- ❒ Olives, pickled (1 piece): 975 mg
- ❒ Chocolate chip cookie (1 piece): 60 mg
- ❒ Canned baked beans (1 cup): 856 mg
- ❒ Salted butter (1 tbsp): 82 mg
- ❒ Nachos with cheese (6–8 pieces): 816 mg
- ❒ French fries (1 large): 328 mg

❐ Barbeque sauce (1 tbsp): 128 mg
❐ Processed cheese (100 g): 1,320 mg

You can see that even by consuming innocent-looking foods like bread, breakfast cereals and nuts, your child can easily cross the recommended sodium allowance per day.

All in the Family: Salt and Its Numerous Nicknames

Salt can be hidden in the garb of other names too, so don't sit easy when you find the word 'salt' missing from the 'nutrition facts' on the label of a product. Sodium may be sitting stealthily there, camouflaged behind its alternate names, such as sodium; sea salt; rock salt; sodium bicarbonate (baking soda); monosodium glutamate (MSG); sodium chloride; brine; sodium saccharin; sodium propionate; sodium nitrite; sodium metabisulphite; sodium erythorbate; disodium EDTA; disodium 5'-guanyla; sodium alginate; sodium ascorbate; sodium benzoate; sodium caseinate; sodium citrate; sodium hydroxide; sodium stearoyl lactylate; sodium sulphite; disodium phosphate; trisodium phosphate; and of course, the chemical name, Na.

Maximum Daily Allowance

According to the National Health Service, UK (NHS, UK) guidelines, the daily recommended amount of salt that children should consume is as follows:

- Under 1 year: less than 1 gram per day
- 1–3 years: 2 grams per day
- 4–6 years: 3 grams per day
- 7–10 years: 5 grams per day
- 11 years and above: 6 grams per day

A Caveat

The next time when you go to the supermarket to buy food stuff for your family, keep the following pointers in mind to avoid buying excessive sodium-infested foods:

What food labels claim	What they actually mean:
Sodium-free	Less than 5 mg sodium per serving
Very low sodium	35 mg or less per serving
Low sodium	140 mg or less per serving
Reduced sodium	Sodium reduced by 25%
Unsalted/no added salt	Made without salt, yet contains sodium that is a natural part of the food itself.

Other pointers to cut down sodium drastically from your child's diet are:

- ❏ Cut back on frequent forays to restaurants, since the dishes there are crammed with salt.
- ❏ Try replacing regular table salt with healthier and unrefined salt such as sea salt or rock salt. While regular salt goes through extensive chemical processing, rock salt and sea salt go through minimal processing.
- ❏ Use your culinary skills for cooking with herbs and spices which have strong flavours and reduce the need for much salt. Spices such as cinnamon, black pepper, nutmeg, mace, parsley, basil, oregano, rosemary, sage, thyme, allspice, oregano, cayenne pepper, bay leaves, garlic powder and lemon juice add aroma and flavours to a dish, reducing the need to add much salt.
- ❏ Break the habit of adding extra table salt to cooked food even if it tastes low on salt. If you control the urge a few times, eating food without the customary shake of the salt cellar will become a habit.
- ❏ Say no to processed/packaged/ready-to-eat foods. They're loaded with sodium.
- ❏ Choose unsalted nuts instead of salted ones.

It's not about total elimination of salt from the diet (which can actually be catastrophic to health), it's about just a little more than a pinch of salt a day, controlling the salt intake down to the recommended level. Most of us eat much more of it than is required on a daily basis.

Combined S-S-F Offenders

Some of the nastiest food offenders are food items which combine two or all three of the bad sources of S–S–Fs in excess. Some of these are:

- ❐ Cakes, cookies, pastries and doughnuts (trans fats, sodium and added sugars)
- ❐ Meat burgers and hotdogs (trans fats, saturated fat and sodium)
- ❐ Ice cream (saturated fats and added sugars)
- ❐ Chicken nuggets, fried chicken (trans fats and sodium)
- ❐ Milkshakes (saturated fat and added sugars)
- ❐ Processed meats like sausages, salami, bacon, frankfurters and deli meats (saturated fat and sodium)
- ❐ Packaged potato wedges/Smileys (trans fats and sodium)
- ❐ French fries (trans fats and sodium)
- ❐ Ketchup (added sugar and sodium)
- ❐ Commercially made popcorn/nachos (trans fats and sodium)

The Verdict

When these three evil charmers are combined to cook up a dish, the epicurean allure of that food is enhanced. Since the sugar-salt-fat trio is highly addictive, the consumption of a food high in these evils increases the dopamine levels in the brain. This further heightens the craving for that food, leaving one wanting more and more of the same. The whole eating experience becomes emotional, especially for children, and lack of gratification could well lead to anxiety. A single sugar-salt-fat laden meal in a restaurant could cover your child's calorie-ration for the entire day or more. So, be smart and don't let your child overindulge in the dreaded trinity—and watch her blossom into a fit and healthy child!

Chapter 8

Food for Thought

A Brain Boosting Diet for Your Child

Most of us want our kids to be the Einsteins of the future. And there certainly is nothing wrong with aspiring to have a brilliant kid. While intelligence may be an innate attribute, one can certainly sharpen mental acuity and enhance cognitive health with a little help from the kitchen. The brain is a hungry organ with an enormous appetite. If you feed it well with certain foods, it will get nourishment and improve its functioning.

There are certain highly effective nutrients that boost memory, academic performance, concentration, problem-solving skills and ameliorate overall brain health. I have picked the following foods as the brain's closest allies.

Top Twelve Highbrow Foods

Oily fish: Oily fish is rich in omega-3 fatty acids that help the brain develop tissue for increasing brain power by boosting energy, enhancing learning ability, increasing mental acuity, improving problem-solving skills and augmenting memory power. The best source of oily fish is salmon. Other fish include trout, mackerel, halibut, tuna, herring, anchovies, sardines, pilchards and kippers. Oily fish is an anti-inflammatory food for the brain. So, lap it up!

Nuts: Push your little one's brain health several notches up by feeding her nuts. They are high in brain-protective compounds, omega-3 and vitamin E, which are necessary for boosting memory and cognitive skills. These omega-3 rich nuts are also loaded with mood-enhancing neurotransmitters that reduce mental stress, which in turn leads to better focus. The brain is better able to think clearly and process information distinctly with such nourishment. Walnuts and almonds are the front-runners as far as these benefits are concerned.

Seeds: Seeds are not only a great source of omega-3, ALA and omega-6 fatty acids and vitamin E, but also a good source of vitamin B_6 and zinc, which are vital for enhancing memory and thinking skills. Great seeds to feed on are pumpkin seeds, flax seeds and sunflower seeds. While flax seeds are a rich source of memory-boosting omega-3 fatty acids, pumpkin seeds contain tryptophan which relaxes the mind and zinc that enhances memory and cognitive skills. Sunflower seeds offer thiamine that improves memory and cognitive functions. They also contain dopamine that increases concentration levels.

Whole-grains: Besides omega-3 fatty acids, the brain also needs energy to function efficiently. To enhance focus on studies, young minds need a steady supply of glucose in their blood, which is then transported to the brain. To reap these benefits, you need to pick whole grains for them, which release glucose slowly into the bloodstream, keeping them mentally sharp through the day. Whole grains are also very rich in B vitamins, iron and magnesium. Give your little one cereals or grains such as brown rice, oatmeal, wheat bran, barley, wheat germ, sprouted grains, multigrain bread, wholewheat pasta and air-popped popcorn, since they contain a high percentage of folate and thiamine that boost the blood flow to the brain. As a result, there is a spike of energy and attention, which is essential for mental alertness.

Eggs: Eggs are a rich source of omega-3 fatty acids and protein. While we know what role omega-3 fatty acids play in the brain, protein is the basic building block of brain cells. It aids in a number of brain functions, improving memory being just one of them. They are also a rich source of tyrosine that enhances mental alertness.

Broccoli: This cruciferous vegetable is a rich source of anti-oxidants and nutrients like lycopene, beta-carotene, vitamin C, vitamin A and vitamin K. All these possess the power to enhance cognitive function, reduce mental stress and improve brainpower. A diet rich in broccoli will keep kids mentally active through the day. Besides, broccoli is also rich in calcium, iron and folic acid, which are also essential for growth of brain tissue.

Avocados: Avocados contain vitamin E that promotes brain health. They help keep the little brains sharp by virtue of the increased blood flow to the brain.

Bananas: They augment the brain chemical called dopamine that helps the brain to focus and stay stimulated for mental activities. Bananas are also rich in vitamin B_6, which helps kids to remain high on energy and boosts concentration levels.

Berries: Eating berries that are chock-full of anti-oxidants is a good way to improve memory and attention, as well as help children solve different tasks. While the ultimate 'brain-berry' is blueberry as it improves motor skills and learning capacity, it is sadly not freely available in India. However, other berries like strawberries, blackberries, cranberries and raspberries are also rich in flavonoids that improve memory recall and have other brain power-enhancing benefits because of their antioxidant content. Like bananas, berries also enhance dopamine levels in the brain, which leads to sharpening of the cognitive skills.

Tomatoes: Lycopene, a potent antioxidant that protects the cells in the brain against the damage caused by free radicals, is abundant in tomatoes. So, feed them to your little ones regularly for the cerebral perks they offer.

Spinach: Folic acid, iron and vitamin E in spinach boost nerve cell health and hence help in concentration.

Water: Nearly three-fourths of the brain is water, which makes this life-giving liquid an essential component for smooth functioning of the brain. When dehydration occurs, the brain releases the hormone cortisol, which constricts the brain cells and tissue, leading to fatigue, mental lethargy and clouded thinking. So, make sure your little one irrigates her grey cells by drinking at least seven to eight glasses of water a day to keep her brain active, sharp and refreshed the entire day.

While the above foods may ace the nutrition charts as the 'Top Twelve Brain Foods', they are definitely not the only choices available to nourish the budding grey cells. There is an assortment of foods available in the market that can help foster the scholar in your child. So, let us categorize these foods nutrient-wise this time round.

Top Mind-hoisting Nutrients

Macronutrients

Omega-3 fatty acids (good fats): These are significant for memory and cognitive performance. Omega-3 fatty acid deficiency can lead to depression, poor memory, mental fatigue and mood swings. Best sources are: oils (olive, canola, soybean, corn, peanut, flaxseed, sesame, almond, sunflower and safflower oil), nuts (hazelnuts, almonds, walnuts, pistachios and cashews), seeds (flaxseeds, sesame and pumpkin), fatty fish (salmon, tuna, mackerel, catfish, herring, anchovies and trout), olives, peanut butter and avocados.

Amino acids (proteins): Protein contains amino acids that are the building blocks of the brain's network and help in the production of neurotransmitters that regulate brain function. These amino acids are responsible for calming the mind, as well as mental alertness and focus. The best sources are: low-fat dairy products like milk, yogurt, cottage cheese, buttermilk and cheese; poultry; eggs; fish and sea food; soy products like tofu, soy milk, soybeans, soy nuggets, soy granules, soy flour; dried beans like kidney beans, garbanzo beans, black-eyed beans, black chana, dried peas; nuts like almonds, pistachios, walnuts, cashews and hazelnuts; seeds like pumpkin seeds, sunflower seeds, chia seeds and flaxseeds.

Dietary fibre (complex carbohydrates): Carbohydrates are broken down into glucose, which is used as a fuel to aid brain activity. By virtue of regulating the brain glucose levels, fibrous carbohydrates (complex carbohydrates) raise mental alertness and lower stress levels. These foods also aid memory and protect the brain from free radical damage. A diet that is low in carbohydrates will most likely lead to brain fog and low energy. The best sources are: wholewheat bread and roti; brown rice; cereals such as oatmeal and broken wheat porridge; whole-wheat pasta; whole grains like bran, soya, pearl millet, cracked wheat, buckwheat, barley, sorghum, chana; lentils and legumes; dried beans like kidney beans, garbanzo beans, black-eyed beans, black chana, dried peas, sprouts; fibrous fruits and vegetables like potato, sweet potato, beans, peas, apple, pear and avocado.

Micronutrients

Vitamin B₁ (Thiamine): Vitamin B1 helps the body's cells to change carbohydrates into energy. This process helps deliver energy to the brain and nervous system. Best sources are: kidney beans, black-eyed beans, lentils, oatmeal, wholewheat, sesame seeds, sunflower seeds, flaxseeds, Brazil nuts, walnuts, pistachios, hazelnuts, salmon, lamb liver, sorghum and broccoli.

Vitamin B₆ (Pyridoxine): The three neurotransmitters in the brain, namely gamma-aminobutyric acid (GABA), dopamine and serotonin need vitamin B_6 for synthesis. This nutrient also boosts energy and heightens concentration levels. The best sources are: soybeans, chickpeas, sesame seeds, sunflower seeds, flaxseeds, cashew nuts, walnuts, pistachios, hazelnuts, peanuts, mackerel, tuna, trout, salmon, halibut, codfish, poultry, lamb liver, banana, wholewheat, broccoli, potato, sweet potato, red capsicum and plantain.

Vitamin B_9 (Folate): This vitamin plays an important role in mental health and other brain functions. The best sources are: soybeans, kidney beans, black-eyed beans, chickpeas, lentils, oatmeal, rice, sesame seeds, sunflower seeds, flaxseeds, walnuts, hazelnuts, peanuts, eggs, turnip greens, potato, peas, beetroot, broccoli, avocado, guava, pomegranate, lamb liver and chicken liver.

Vitamin B_{12} (Cobalamin): Vitamin B_{12} helps in maintenance of the central nervous system and improves cognitive functioning of the brain. Best sources are: mackerel, tuna, trout, salmon, halibut, herring, sardines, mutton, lamb liver, chicken liver, eggs, soy milk, yogurt, cheese and cottage cheese.

Vitamin C (ascorbic acid): Vitamin C plays an important role in brain health as it synthesizes the neurotransmitter called serotonin, which is also known as 'the happy molecule'. Vitamin C-rich foods are also potent antioxidants that facilitate proper blood flow to the brain. This in turn supplies more oxygen to the brain cells, making the brain function optimally. Best sources are: apricots, banana, mango, oranges, muskmelon, honeydew melon, papaya, guava, kiwi, watermelon, avocado, plums, grapefruit, strawberries, pomegranate, raspberries, pineapple, gooseberries, lemon, brussels sprouts, green beans, spinach, broccoli, mustard greens, turnip greens, beet greens, pumpkin, capsicum, tomatoes, potato, sweet potato, cabbage, red cabbage, cauliflower, peas, onions, bok choy, okra, jackfruit, radish, ridge gourd/zucchini, coriander, plantain, lotus stem, colacassia leaves, dil leaves and kidney beans.

Vitamin E: Vitamin E is a robust antioxidant that works toward nerve cell protection. Best sources are: nuts like almonds, Brazil nuts, hazelnuts and peanuts; oils like canola, olive, sunflower, safflower and soybean; sunflower seeds; vegetables like mustard greens, turnip greens, pumpkin, red peppers; and fruits like mango and papaya.

Vitamin K: Vitamin K is an active participant in nervous tissue biochemistry and improves cognitive functioning of the brain. Best sources are: soybeans, pistachios, hazelnuts, avocado, kiwi, pomegranate, figs, prunes, dried peaches, green beans, mustard greens, turnip greens, beet greens, spinach, broccoli, carrots, cabbage, cauliflower, bok choy, brussels sprouts, peas, okra, lettuce, asparagus and oils like canola, olive, safflower and soybean.

Iron: Iron plays a very crucial role in the development of the brain during the early years, impacting behaviour and intelligence. The consequences of iron deficiency is grave in children, as it can upset their normal intellectual development. The deficiency could also lead to attention-deficit or hyperactivity disorder and can severely affect the IQ of a child. Best sources are: meats like mutton liver, beef, chicken liver; eggs; fish like halibut, salmon and tuna; spinach; dried fruits like raisins, peaches, apricots and prunes; beans like kidney beans, black-eyed beans, soybeans, chickpeas; lentils; tofu; whole grains like buckwheat, wholewheat, barley, sorghum and oats; wholewheat bread, seeds like pumpkin seeds, sunflower seeds, flaxseeds and sesame seeds; nuts like almonds, walnuts, cashews, pistachios, hazelnuts, peanuts and fortified cereals.

Iodine: This nutrient is needed for synthesis of the thyroid hormone, which helps to keep the cerebral cells healthy in children. Iodine deficiency can lead to reduced alertness and lowered IQ. Best sources are: iodized salt, cod fish, tuna, shrimp, yogurt, milk, cheddar cheese, sea vegetables and seaweeds like kelp.

Diet Pointers for Exam Time

Before concluding this chapter, it's pertinent for me to dole out a few important tips about eating habits around exam time that have worked well for my son all through his school years. Although food alone may not be enough to blot out stress resulting from studies, smart eating can definitely blunt the blow and ease out a considerable amount of anxiety. Take a look at these pointers:

❑ Make sure that your child eats all his meals on time at regular intervals. It will keep his stomach full and keep him from craving food that can be a big distraction. Timely hunger gratification also ensures that your child doesn't start losing focus due to lack of energy and a foggy brain.

❑ Never let your child skip breakfast. Whether the exam is in the morning or afternoon, a good breakfast keeps energy levels up for most part of the day. It should be a healthy combination of carbohydrates and protein to keep the body and mind alert and to hike up concentration levels.

❑ Ensure that the apple of your eye drinks enough water at regular intervals throughout the day. This will keep her from feeling fatigued and low on concentration.

❑ Offer a light meal to your child before the exam hour. Overstuffing the tummy could make him lethargic and drowsy during the exam. Just ensure that his pre-exam meal comprises carbohydrate to fuel his brain, protein to calm it and a bit of the good fats to boost cognitive performance.

❑ Keep dried fruits, nuts, or trail-mix handy near her study table. This will ensure she doesn't reach out for junk food, which could cause discomfort to some kids during exam time. Dried fruits and nuts are good sources of energy and can whet mental agility.

❏ Restrict your child from drinking coffee and other caffeinated drinks on a regular basis. These have an adverse effect on the appetite. Caffeine may stimulate the brain temporarily and help the child stay alert, but it also suppresses the feeling of hunger, which is not healthy. Too much caffeine can even make children feel jittery where the body may feel alert, but the mind is sluggish.

❏ Offer your child ginger tea, chamomile tea, or any other herbal infusion for an instant 'pick-me-up' feeling.

❏ During exam time, ensure that your child only eats foods she is used to consuming. Experimenting with new foods, however healthy, is a big no-no. It can upset the stomach or cause cramps in case the food doesn't suit the child. This is not a chance you would want to take with her exams on.

The Verdict

Deficiency of the above-mentioned vital macronutrients and micronutrients could result in impairment of mental growth in children, thwarting their brains' ability to function properly. During heavy academic pressure days, good nutrition really helps children maintain optimal concentration and mental energy, even as it equips them to deal positively with the extended study hours.

It's a delight for me as a nutritionist to watch the transformation of my young clients. With a little tweaking of their diet, they move from weary and washed-out pupils with no will to study, to mentally agile and invigorated children.

So, just add these superfoods to your kids' daily diet and witness a marked improvement in their focus and mental alacrity, which should naturally translate into better grades!

Chapter 9

Fuel for the Fitness Fanatics

Calorie Requirements of Young Athletes and Physically Active Kids

It's D-day for Rohan. He is all kitted up for his tennis game and ready to go.

- ✓ Babolat Racquet: Check!
- ✓ Adidas Barricades: Check!
- ✓ Nike shorts and tee: Check!
- ✓ Wrist bands: Check!
- ✓ Racquet strings tightened: Check!
- ✓ Overgrip fastened: Check!
- ✓ Shocker fixed: Check!
- ✓ Water: Check!
- ✓ Gatorade: Check!

What more could an ace player like Rohan ask for to win the tennis tournament? Besides, he had practised diligently all month. The game starts. He appears to have an edge. But gradually, he fumbles and loses the handle. What started well in the first round, turned unexpectedly disastrous by round three. He is totally drained and burnt-out by game four, and eventually loses the game. What could have led to this debacle? After all, he had worked hard and had all that he needed. I get on with my investigation, and an hour later I present the diagnosis. Here it is:

Rohan was exercising hard every day, but his diet did not match up to his exertion levels. It was deficient in essential calories like complex carbohydrates and proteins. So, while he was helping himself from the outside with enough practice, he wasn't getting enough help from within.

Children who play sports or exercise regularly undoubtedly have a substantially increased calorie need. In simple words, they may need more performance-enhancing food because they burn more calories as athletes due to exerting themselves for extended hours of play. If your sporty moppet is well-nourished with an athlete's diet, he is sure to play better because he will have more energy and stamina, coupled with mentally agility. Rohan, on the other hand, ate the diet of a normal child, which was not compatible with his body's requirements. Hence, he lost stamina and eventually lost the game.

Benefits of Eating Right As a Jock

A good diet planned according to the nutritional needs of a sportsman's body builds endurance to train for longer durations; boosts energy levels to play efficiently; prevents fatigue during exercise; improves muscle strength to take on the rigours of intense exercise; accelerates muscle recovery from wear and tear after strenuous workouts; and strengthens bones and joints for weight-bearing exercises.

It also sharpens mental agility and improves concentration to strategize and focus on the game; braces the body for the rigours of high-intensity workouts; enhances the body's immune system so that the time for play is not hampered by illnesses; and raises the metabolic rate of the body, which curbs unwanted kilos that could hinder speed and agility needed by athletes.

Moreover, a good 'sportsman' diet which includes bone and muscle strengthening nutrients reduces the risk of sports injuries. It also lowers the risk of heat stroke and dehydration, which are very dangerous for a sports person.

Estimated amounts of calories needed by physically active children vis-à-vis sedentary kids

Gender	Age	Sedentary	Active
Female	4–8	1,200	1,400–1,800
	9–13	1,600	1,800–2,200
	14–18	1,800	2,400
Male	4–8	1,400	1,600–2,000
	9–13	1,800	2,000–2,600
	14–18	2,200	2,800–3,200

*These levels are based on Estimated Energy Requirements (EER) from the Institute of Medicine Dietary Reference Intakes macronutrients report, 2002, calculated by gender, age and activity level for reference-sized individuals.

Specific Nutrients Needed by Athletes and Physically Active Children

Macronutrients

Proteins: Young athletes expend much more energy during intense physical activity than sedentary kids and therefore, their bodies need extra protein for strengthening muscles and for recovery from post-exercise muscle soreness.

Proteins are found in lean meat, chicken breast, poultry, eggs, fish, seafood, low fat dairy products, soy products, dried beans, lentils, nuts, seeds and peanut butter.

Warning: A very high-protein diet can be counter-productive for young athletes because proteins are generally hiked in the diet at the cost of carbohydrates. We know by now that carbohydrates are the main source of providing energy to the body and keep kids from burning out.

Complex carbohydrates: Carbohydrates are the main source of energy for the body and athletes need them in larger quantities.

These are found in wholewheat bread, wholewheat roti, brown rice, wholewheat pasta, cereals like oatmeal, broken wheat porridge, wheat flakes and muesli; lentils, legumes, dried beans, dried fruits, homemade granola, energy bars; fibrous vegetables like potato, sweet potato, beans and peas; and fruits like apple, banana, orange and pear.

Simple carbohydrates: These help in preventing dehydration and fatigue, which can impair an athlete's training and performance. Simple carbohydrates are best used judiciously on a need basis only. Sporty children who exercise for more than ninety minutes or play intense sports like sprints, tennis, squash, or football for a minimum of one hour, may consume simple carbohydrates.

These are mildly sweetened sports drinks, lightly sweetened lemonade (preferably with honey) and diluted fresh fruit juices without added sugar. Most fruits, dried fruits like dates, apricots, black currants and raisins; some vegetables like sweet potato, beetroot and carrot; and milk are also good sources of natural and simple sugar.

Good fats: Fats, too, are a big energy source for young athletes. While carbohydrates are the main energy source for kids during short-duration or lower-intensity exercise, fats are the prime fuel source during longer-duration or higher-intensity exercise.

Good fats are found in cooking oils like olive and canola, nuts like almonds and walnuts, seeds like flaxseeds, sesame and pumpkin, fatty fish like salmon, tuna and mackerel, dairy products and peanut butter.

Micronutrients

Calcium: All young athletes need strong bones to be able to play strenuous sports. If the bones are weak, intense physical activity can cause stress fractures. Adequate calcium in the diet helps build strong bones, prevents stress injuries and arrests a steep decline in bone density in later years.

Good food sources of calcium are: milk and other dairy products, soy milk, tofu, broccoli, spinach, mustard greens, fish like salmon and sardines, ragi, wholewheat, sesame seeds, flaxseeds, dried fruits and almonds.

Iron: Iron deficiency can lead to anaemia in which the body manufactures fewer red blood cells. The oxygen flow through the blood to the entire body is curtailed. This oxygen restriction leads to fatigue and lower concentration levels. When the concentration levels drop, the sports performance drops too, as a consequence of physical and mental fatigue. Menstruation could be another possible cause of iron deficiency anaemia in girls. Therefore, foods rich in iron are needed for correction of this ailment.

Good food sources of iron are: mutton/chicken liver, salmon, tuna, eggs, spinach, dried fruits, dried beans, dals, tofu, whole grains, oats, wholewheat bread, nuts, seeds, peanut butter and fortified cereals.

Magnesium: Besides being involved in over 300 biological functions in the body, magnesium is needed for muscle contraction and relaxation and in energy production. If there is a deficiency of this mineral in children who play sports, it could lead to muscle cramps leading to a decline in muscle performance.

Good dietary sources of magnesium are: spinach, potato, sweet potato, whole-grain bread, wholewheat, barley, brown rice, oats, dried beans, dals, figs, seeds, nuts, peanut butter, eggs and fish like halibut and mackerel.

Zinc: This mineral is extremely vital for athletic performance. It is because zinc directly affects thyroid hormone levels, which in turn affect the basal metabolic rate of the body. Since the thyroid hormone is crucial for the proper functioning of every cell in the body, a poor zinc status can affect proper protein synthesis, energy production, heart and lung function, repair of muscle tissue, strength and endurance. It can even affect the immune system of the body. Sufficient evidence shows that zinc deficiency can bring down physical performance as well as the general health of an athlete.

The best zinc sources are: oats; seeds like sesame seeds, pumpkin seeds, sunflower seeds and flaxseeds; nuts like almonds, walnuts, peanuts and pistachios; peanut butter; dried peaches; lamb liver; and cheese.

Vitamin D: This is one of the most essential nutrients for strong bones. It is responsible for adequate calcium absorption. The sports performance of children could be greatly affected by vitamin D deficiency, as this inadequacy is very likely to lead to bone pain and acute muscle weakness. In cases of substantial vitamin D deficiency, dietary sources alone are insufficient for recovery. Athletes would benefit from taking vitamin D supplements on a physician's advice, based on their blood test report.

Dietary sources of vitamin D are: cod liver oil, fish like halibut, herring, mackerel and sardines, egg yolks, mushrooms, fortified milk and fortified orange juice.

B vitamins: B vitamins are a versatile group of eight essential vitamins that play important roles in cell metabolism. Together, they are needed in good measure for maximum energy production during physical performance for the repair of muscle tissue, protein synthesis and production of red blood cells. Vitamin B deficiency can result in anaemia that can further lead to muscle weakness, lack of energy, numbness, light-headedness and impaired physical and mental growth. Regular episodes of these could impede the athletic performance seriously. Vitamin B deficiency is generally more common amongst vegetarians.

Good sources of B vitamins are: cereals, dried beans, seeds, nuts, peanut butter, fish, dried fruits, lentils, fruits like banana, avocado, guava and pomegranate, soymilk, leafy green vegetables, root vegetables, dairy products, meat and eggs.

Vitamin C: Very vigorous and prolonged exercise can lead to oxidative stress because of free radical damage in the body. This can ruin physical performance to a great extent. In such a case, an antioxidant like vitamin C is crucial in salvaging the situation and increasing immunity against these harmful free radicals.

Good sources of vitamin C are: vegetables like broccoli, cabbage, capsicum, squash, tomatoes, cauliflower, spinach, white potatoes, sweet potato, mustard greens, turnip greens, beet greens, peas, cabbage, green beans, pumpkin and onions; fruits like orange, strawberries, lemons, banana, plums, pomegranate, papaya, guava, kiwi, cantaloupe, honeydew melon, mango, watermelon, raspberries, pineapple, apricot and Indian gooseberry; kidney beans and lamb liver.

Other Essential Nutrients

Water: Children have a greater need for fluids than adults. Kids who play intense sports are more likely to suffer from a heat stroke or dehydration than adults in the same circumstances if they do not hydrate themselves well—because children cannot regulate their body temperature the way adults can. Perspiration leads to water loss through the pores of the skin. Sometimes when the exercise is very intense or is done in hot and humid weather, the water loss may be substantial and may lead to overheating of the body or dehydration. *Severe dehydration can be dangerous and sometimes fatal too.* This is why our blooming sportspersons need to drink water before, during and after exercise. So, don't forget to pack an extra water bottle for your child the next time he steps out for a sports session.

Although, water is the best bet to hydrate young bodies, consuming the following coolers (as mentioned earlier) is beneficial during and after rigorous exercise, when exercising intensely for more than an hour or when exercising in hot and humid weather. The list includes lightly sweetened sports drinks;

lightly sweetened and salted lemonade; diluted fresh fruit juices; and coconut water.

These fluids will not only hydrate but also replenish the electrolytes lost through perspiration such as magnesium, potassium, sodium, phosphorus, calcium and chloride.

So how much H_2O is sufficient? According to WebMD.com, the hydration schedule for active children should be:

Before exercise: 16 ounces (about two cups) two hours before the activity.

During exercise: 4–6 ounces every fifteen to twenty minutes.

After exercise: Ideally, a child should be weighed before the exercise begins and then at the finish. For each pound of water weight lost, 20 ounces of water should be consumed.

Note: Check out the chapters on macronutrients, micronutrients and hydration for in-depth and age-wise dietary recommendations of each of the above-mentioned nutrients.

Food Regime on the Final Event Day

It's very crucial to plan your child's diet meticulously for the final day of a sports event to optimize his performance and to prevent food-related distress during the event that could topple his apple cart. So, here's how you should plan his intake before, after and during the sports session.

Pre-exercise Meal

A meal comprising a balanced combination of high carbs, moderate protein and good fats along with the right amount of fluids two to three hours before the exercise session, will provide adequate energy and nourishment to the muscles to perform well. It will also help to keep hunger from interfering with the exercise.

For proper and timely digestion of the pre-exercise meal to

avoid stomach discomfort during the session, ensure the following:

❏ Meals should be low in fibre and fat as these take longer than carbs to digest.
❏ Avoid heavy meals as some kids can get jittery just before their events. A light and simple meal can prevent discomfort.
❏ Meals should not be eaten too close to the exercise/sports event. A gap of two to three hours is ideal.
❏ Children should keep sipping water/sports drinks in hot and humid weather until the start of the sporting event. However, they need to avoid guzzling large quantities to prevent discomfort from the liquid sloshing in the stomach.

Ideal pre-exercise meals would include:

Fluids: I'd recommend around 230 ml to 250 ml of water; 250 ml of low-fat or skimmed milk; 250 ml of diluted fresh fruit juice; 250 ml of a sports drink; a glass of coconut water; or a glass of low-fat lassi sweetened with a little honey

Carbs-protein combo meals: Some meal ideas include a fruit salad with yogurt and a few nuts; fruit and yogurt smoothie; banana with milk or yogurt; fresh fruit yogurt; pasta in red sauce with or without boiled chicken; whole grain (vegetable, paneer or chicken) sandwich; grilled fish; oatmeal, muesli or wheat flakes with milk; fruit milkshake; brown or white rice with dal; broken wheat porridge with milk; grilled chicken breast with mashed potato; boiled eggs, single fried eggs, omelette or scrambled eggs on wholewheat toasts; sprouts and fruit salad; sprouts and vegetable salad; boiled chickpeas salad; whole moong, yellow moong or besan chillas; banana or apple slices with peanut butter; peanut butter on wholewheat toasts; and wholewheat pita bread or chips with hummus or other low-fat dips.

Refuelling During Exercise

In sports that last more than an hour, such as football, it is crucial to replace electrolytes lost through sweat. Some foods containing carbohydrates and electrolytes that can be consumed during sports are sports drinks (lightly sweetened); diluted fresh fruit juices; coconut water; banana; sports bars (low sugar); boiled or sweet potato; and wholewheat bread slices with honey.

Fuelling Post-exercise

For fast muscle recovery and to replenish the electrolytes lost from the body through excessive perspiration, your child should remember to do the following:

❑ Slowly drink enough water to refuel the tired body. It is not necessary to consume a sports drink after a competition. Instead, cold water, coconut water and juicy oranges with or without a little salt are great to replenish lost electrolytes and restore energy.

❑ Consume a high-protein snack within forty-five minutes of hard, taxing exercise session.

❑ Consume a meal which consists of high carbs and moderate proteins about two hours after the exercise session.

Quick Tips for Fledgling Athletes

Here are some more tips related to food for our young and aspiring athletes:

Power-up the performance with a healthy snack: Active kids have to keep themselves constantly fuelled with energy. To ensure energy reserves all day, they need to munch on small snacks every two to three hours. While a lot of snack ideas have already been given (Read 'Ideal pre-exercise meals' in this chapter), a few more healthy snack ideas are homemade low-fat granola; homemade sports bar, energy bar or muesli bar; trail-mix (almonds, peanuts, dried cranberries, raisins, dates, sunflower seeds); fresh fruit; dried fruits; mixed nuts; poha with peanuts or peas; semolina upma; low-fat cheese slice; low-fat cheese on wholewheat toast; chopped vegetables with hummus dip; wholewheat crackers; buttermilk; boiled corn; and yes, a hot chocolate drink.

Avoid high sugar foods: Sodas, ice creams, concentrated juices, chocolates and candy bars just before the sporting event may give your little athlete instant energy, but it is likely to recede as fast, leaving him feeling totally drained. So, avoid those empty calories.

No skipping meals: Make sure your young one does not skip meals. Eating three main meals and two to three smaller snack-meals regularly each day can stabilize blood sugar. This in turn will prevent the following issues that could negatively affect performance: binge eating due to sugar cravings; indigestion; stomach cramps due to gas build-up; and plunging energy levels.

Avoid new foods on the event day: We know that variety is the spice of life, but make sure not to experiment with new foods the night before or on the day of the event. New foods may not sit well in the child's stomach and may cause diarrhoea/constipation/stomach ache/stomach cramps, which may affect performance. Ideally, offer her new foods on practice days to ascertain if the foods suit her stomach.

A big 'no' to caffeinated drinks: Young bodies cannot handle high levels of caffeine. Caffeinated energy drinks increase the heart rate, may lead to an irregular heartbeat and may even jack up the blood pressure. In a heightened state like this, children are likely to lose focus on the game and end up jittery. Even worse, instead of hydrating the athletes, caffeinated energy drinks end up dehydrating them. So, it is best to avoid meddling with the heart just for a little kick that cannot live up to its expectations.

Sports Drinks Versus Energy Drinks

While sports drinks are not essential for active children to provide energy for everyday play, they may be beneficial for those who play intense sports that last ninety minutes or more. Sports drinks contain carbohydrates (glucose) and electrolytes like sodium, potassium, calcium and chloride, which together replenish energy and electrolytes lost through sweat.

Energy drinks , on the other hand, are crammed to the brim with caffeine that is too much for young kids to handle. They contain too much sugar that can cause unnecessary weight gain. Far from being a source of sustained energy for young athletes, energy drinks are known to cause uneven heartbeats, jitters, high blood pressure, reduced concentration, headaches, upset stomach and a host of other fallouts. The stark reality is that energy drinks pose a real health risk for kids and teens and should be avoided.

The Verdict

Now that you're fully clued in on how to feed your sporty little devil, pump up his diet according to his physical activity levels, play duration and the weather. Then watch him enjoy his game and finish as strong and energetic as he was at the start!

Chapter 10
Beyond Mamma's Kitchen
Eating Right when Eating Out

Almost all the nutritionists, doctors and wellness experts across the globe will caution you that dining out is a grave evil, a sin with no retribution other than zipping up your mouth, only to open it occasionally to ingest the oppressive diet that bans all epicurean treats from venturing even remotely close to your taste buds. It sure looks like a dismal picture. Need the activity of satiating hunger be so joyless and grim? I mean, seriously? I think not! An occasional foray to your favourite restaurant or bakery is certainly not a crime. When you're regularly following a balanced diet, indulging in your favourite foods occasionally only helps you to stay on the healthy eating track. Mind you, I recommend eating out only sparingly, which according to me means eating out not more than once a week (once in ten days is even better).

Talking about children, this advice is even more relevant. If adults can crave for their favourites and indulge themselves, it's only fair that kids be allowed treats now and then too. This way it's more likely that they will mostly stick to eating homemade healthy meals, without killing the fun and excitement associated with eating.

By encouraging your children to eat out once in a while, I am definitely not implying that the eat-out spree turn recklessly unhealthy. Whoever said that kids only want to eat burgers, pizzas, hot dogs and doughnuts? They may surprise you by experimenting with new, albeit healthy, foods with a little guidance from you.

You can definitely create a balance in which your child gets to eat her favourite foods without the overheads of a terribly unhealthy diet chart. Here are some pointers that can help you make wise choices for your child while dining out.

Tips for Fine Dining

Choose the restaurant wisely: Avoid buffet meals. Buffets can upset the calorie balance gravely. The general tendency is to get the money's worth and hence, parents push their children for refills, asking them to try *everything* they can lay their eyes on. I have often witnessed parents pestering their children to try all the desserts displayed on the buffet table, regardless of whether the child is stuffed and ready to throw up!

Also, avoid eating joints that only serve fast foods that are extremely unhealthy such as pizza, burger, hot dogs, doughnuts, French fries, greasy wraps and so on. This leaves no scope to opt for comparatively healthy dishes in the face of a glut of tempting but unhealthy junk food to choose from.

Ensure your child doesn't leave home hungry: If you have plans to take your child out for a meal, make sure that she has eaten all the meals of that day properly before the outing. This will keep her hunger satiated and her blood sugar in control. This in turn will regulate unreasonable cravings in the restaurant for high-calorie sugary or fried foods like doughnuts, French fries and creamy desserts.

Opt for grilled, boiled, baked, roasted, steamed and stir-fried dishes: Ask the chef for dishes cooked using healthy techniques. Do not hesitate to ask about the cooking oil and the ingredients used, if the description of the dish on the menu card is ambiguous. It doesn't hurt to be a little chatty and assertive sometimes for the sake of your kids' well-being.

Once you get clarity on the cooking technique of each dish, avoid dishes with the following descriptions: pan-fried, deep-fried or batter-fried; crispy or crispy honey; glazed; Alfredo; Florentine. These dishes are loaded with saturated fats that are not only dangerous for the heart but can also lead to obesity. Preferably, choose dishes cooked in canola or olive oil instead of those made in butter, ghee, margarine and shortening.

Slash the portions: Kids have small tummies, so why order an independent dish for them? And that's not all. We nag them to mop up their plates. As if it were not enough that the portion sizes of popular junk foods like burgers and pizzas are ever expanding. Feasting on huge portions of unhealthy foods is one of the major causes of childhood obesity. Therefore, order small portions for your little ones. I assure you that their little tummies would be satisfied much before you think.

Junk the extras: High-fat add-ons like layers of cheese, salted butter, ketchup, soya sauce, other processed sauces, creamy spreads and dips like coleslaw, sour cream and mayonnaise add extra sugar, fat and salt calories to the meal. This, in turn, adds to the risk of adult-onset diabetes, hypertension and obesity. Opt for dips and spreads that use hung curd, olive oil, mint, coriander leaves, tomatoes and vinegar. Sauces like salsa and mustard are fine too.

Tone down that sweet tooth: Very few foods match up to the wickedness of a sweet and creamy dessert. It's a given that most children have a major sweet fixation rather than a craving for salty food. However, it is this addiction for sugary treats that can wreck a child's healthy diet. Sugar-laden foods are the main offenders of good health as they're loaded with empty calories that often lead to diabetes or obesity. If your child wants sweet treats like most children do, don't deny him these sweet pleasures but be smart. Just opt for the healthier choices and avoid foods which use various sweet syrups, whipped cream and icing. So, you need to avoid creamy cakes and pastries (with and without icing), doughnuts, sugary tarts, mousses, cookies and so on. Instead, opt for desserts like freshly made fruit custard, sorbets, fruit yogurt or parfaits.

Pull the brakes on salt: Salt is a taste-enhancer and therefore, used rather generously at restaurants. However, too much salt can lead to water retention and a heightened risk of hypertension in children. Invariably, dishes such as burgers, pizzas, hot dogs, soups, fried starters, French fries, Indian curries and Chinese food are loaded with salt. Any chance of ordering a dish with normal sodium is thwarted by the addition of extras such as cheese, butter, ketchup, other processed sauces, spreads and dips, all of which are brimming with salt. So, prevent your little one from asking for these extras to make eating out a safer bet.

Extras on the side: If rich and creamy sauces, dips and dressings are unavoidable, ask for them separately on the side and make sure your child eats them sparingly.

Beat red meat: Meats like mutton, beef and bacon contain a lot of bad cholesterol. White meats like chicken, fish and poultry are leaner and healthier to indulge in.

Banish that drink: A foray to an eating joint for children generally means a favourite platter accompanied with a can of fizzy drink. Little do parents realize that these sweetened drinks add quite a few sweet-but-empty calories to their daily children's diet. If the kids must have a beverage to accompany their meal, water is the best choice. The other winners on the list are low-fat milk drink, buttermilk, fresh fruit juice (occasional only), vegetable juice, fresh lemonade and coconut water.

Balance the meal: If you have to treat your child to a meal outside, try to choose dishes that offer a balance of the following: lean protein like fish, chicken breast, dried beans, lentils, soy products like tofu and soy milk; complex carbohydrates like wholewheat bread or roti, brown rice, wholewheat pasta and sweet potato; good fats like olive or canola oil; vegetables and/or fruits.

Pan the platter: Avoid the platters in restaurants as they are big enough for almost three people to share, unless you are ordering for the family.

Cast the appetizer away: An appetizer in popular eating joints is anything but what its name suggests—a small snack before the main meal to stimulate hunger. Appetizers these days are big enough to glut the tummy and satisfy hunger completely. So if you have ordered one for your child, it's not imperative to order a complete main course. Or else, shun the appetizer in favour of the main meal.

Root for the humble 'clear soup': Choose clear soups over thick refined flour-cream- or cornflour-based soups. Thick soups can be very high on calories which come from fattening ingredients like refined flour, cornflour and cream. There are more than a few options for light, healthy and low-calorie soups such as clear chicken soup, wonton soup, lemon grass chicken soup, lentil soup, vegetable broth and minestrone soup.

The Verdict

If you consciously follow the above tenets while planning a meal in a restaurant for your child, you will not upset their child's health cart. In fact, you're most likely to return home guilt-free, knowing that you allowed your child to indulge in her favourite meal while keeping the choices as healthy as is possible in a restaurant. Your little one, too, will come back satiated after a memorable meal. Now, that's what I call a win-win situation! What say?

Chapter 11

Fat Boy Slim, Mission Possible

Dealing with Childhood Obesity

The year was 1999. Life was perfect! I had a great job in the Indian Navy as an executive officer, a wonderfully supportive husband and the cutest little two-year-old one could ever wish for! I had a doting nanny to tend to my baby and spoil him silly while I would be busy at work. Could I have asked for more? I guess not, for I felt completely blessed. So what if I had too many irons in the fire! My days were committed to my naval job, while my evenings were assigned to my MBA classes; and whatever little else was left of the night was split up between my MBA assignments, nursing and mollycoddling my little brat and catching up on sleep. But my child's nanny was truly God's largesse—what would I have done without her? She filled up for me by taking complete care of him. Yes, she fed him like crazy the whole day and I wasn't complaining (like a typically guilty mother who has little time for her baby). The proof was there for all to see—my baby looked like an irresistibly cute stuffed toy.

My north Indian relatives (parents and in-laws included) were beaming with pride for I had passed the test of being a loving mother with flying colours for raising a 'very healthy' child. And if they found the diet lacking in 'important nutrients' (read ghee, butter, cream, full-fat milk, sugar), the nanny would be given a crash course by them in cookery to make good the 'deficiency'.

It was a golden period of my life when I felt like a star. So what if it was a borrowed halo from my baby's head! I was basking in my child's glory, brimming with self-worth, as if I were the world's 'Mommy No.1' for nurturing an 'enormously healthy' toddler. My friends, acquaintances, relatives and even passers-by couldn't resist pulling the cheeks of my incredibly cute baby. Wherever we went, he was clearly the show-stopper with his strikingly roly-poly body, chubby cheeks that hopelessly drooped southwards, a multi-layered chin, tubby thighs, butterball buns and a rotund tummy to match. Well, a plump, ruddy child meant a 'well-nourished and healthy' child to me. At least that's what I thought many moons ago.

Cut to 2001. I slam the door open and rush out of my son's paediatrician's clinic, tears rolling down my cheeks. Disbelief was writ large on my face. Could I have been so naive to have completely missed the writing on the wall? Yes, I had been a complete feather-brain! The bubble of my blissful delusion had just been ruthlessly burst by the doctor when he pronounced my son 'OBESE'! That was not all. He reprimanded me for regularly 'overstuffing' my hapless baby till his little stomach revolted in protest. Just to give you the background: I had taken my little one to the doctor since he suffered from an upset tummy ever so often. No marks for guessing what the cause was! The doctor opened my unheeding eyes to the perils of raising an obese child when he rattled off a list of maladies that a child could be prone to early in life, such as diabetes, high blood pressure and high cholesterol. The list was alarming.

Suddenly it all made sense! While I was away at work, the nanny was going overboard with her feeding duty. She probably fed him till he was ready to throw up! It was a moment of epiphany for me! It was time to introspect. I was guilty of neglecting my duties as a mother and was remorseful about my complacency in assuming that all was well. I can't deny that I was cautioned from time to time about the upset little tummy, but failed to take heed.

So when my husband came home that evening, all I said to him in distress was, 'Honey, I blew up the kid!' Yes, that's what I had done to my little one—a big disservice! And all the while I was thinking I was 'conserving his cuteness' by ensuring that he maintained a 'more than healthy' weight.

Cut to the present. Needless to say, I turned much wiser and more well-informed after this historic dressing-down. The revelation by the doctor had rattled my cage, leaving me unnerved. I felt angry with myself. This impelled me to read up extensively on childhood obesity. It's not that I just stopped at firing the search engine with my unceasing queries; I wasn't satisfied until I earned myself a fellowship in applied nutrition, which helped me make peace with myself. I worked diligently on my child's diet and fitness (he was my first client). The realization had dawned upon me that my baby was eating way beyond the admissible calories per day for his age, which I was quick to cut to size. Now I feed him fewer calories but every three hours.

Not ensuring that his physical activity was adequate was another blunder. I redressed it by enrolling him for tennis and taekwondo classes, which he resisted wholeheartedly initially. Soon, he had no choice but to go willingly for the fitness classes as I did not cave in to his resistance. As of today, he loves his tennis classes, swims as often as he can, does free hand body-weight exercises and runs 5–10 kilometres whenever he can. The outcome? He is a strapping eighteen-year-old lad with a lean, muscular body. (Though I can't deny that I miss pinching the two blubbers of flesh hanging on either side of his face!). He is fit enough to inspire his male friends and my instinct tells me, a few girls too. Today, he receives compliments, but the context has altered entirely. Every time someone lauds him for his fit body, he gives me a glance loaded with gratitude. And I pass on that gratitude in spirit to the doctor who jolted me into initiating the positive change.

My reminiscences from the annals of my personal history have been penned here to let you know that 'I've been there, done that'. I started out as a reckless, ignorant mother and have ended up being a well-informed, thoughtful one. My new-found wisdom prompts me to reiterate the crucial fact yet again: 'An overweight child is NOT a healthy child'!

'The rise of child obesity has placed the health of an entire generation at risk,' said Tom Vilsack, the US secretary of agriculture, which sums up my view further.

Volumes have been written on the dangers of child obesity and the internet is abuzz about the increasing onset of lifestyle diseases in young children. Despite living in this era of information overload, many of us consciously or unconsciously, tend to dismiss this verdict as balderdash. Parents continue to languish in the comfort of the moth-balled belief that a plump child is a healthy one and should be cherished for being so.

The aim of this book is not to unveil path-breaking and pristine research on the topic of child obesity. It is an attempt to remove the layer of disinformation and create awareness amongst parents with half-baked wisdom in this domain, by telling them it is possible to bring up a healthy child by following a well-thought-out diet and fitness plan. I accomplish this through my professional knowledge and personal experiences. These concepts have been tried and tested by me while raising my son and validated by the parents of many children who have come to me for nutrition advice over the years.

Reasons for Obesity

Obesity has more than doubled in children and quadrupled in adolescents in the past thirty years. An estimated 50–70 per cent of obese children will turn into obese adults according to the forecast. After conceding that childhood obesity is a worldwide epidemic, let's sniff out and hunt down the culprits of this malaise. While the list of offenders is long, there are two prime accused.

Primary Offenders

Overeating: A flawed diet is a major cause of piling up fat calories in children. Regular consumption of junk food such as chips, nachos, cookies, cakes, candy, soda, burgers and pizzas (the list is ever-increasing) will most definitely lead to undesirable weight gain. Not only these, but some of our 'desi' food choices too can wreak havoc with young bodies. Included in this list are aloo-puri, chhole-bhature, ghee-dripping halwa, greasy aloo parantha, fried aloo tikki and shahi tukda, to name a few. Many parents go overboard in feeding their children extra fatty, junk food. All they worry about is whether the object of their affection still has some room left to shove in more food in the small belly beyond its normal capacity. Perhaps for them, the indication for a full and 'not hungry any more' tummy must mean that the child burps and belches and wiggles and winces in discomfort with a tummy-ache resulting from overeating. This is the only way for the stomach to stage an angry protest against torture by its owner.

It's really amusing and disconcerting at the same time, to observe the behaviour of a few parents at various celebrations they attend. They can be spotted piling up their children's plates till food is ready to fall off from atop the food mountain! Their logic is to make their child try out most of the delicious dishes laid out for the guests, perhaps because of the instinctive fear of *'kal party ho na ho'*. The only problem is that the dishes to be savoured can number up to a hundred if not more. This overindulgence and not eating just to satiate one's hunger leads to a calorie overload, which is far in excess of the daily calorific need of the child.

Under-exercising: While the calorie intake of children has generally shot up, their physical activity levels have shrunk with shocking speed. Around 67 per cent children in the country spend less than one hour in physical activity. In the modern high-tech era, computers, television, video games, mobile phones and tablets have conspired to keep kids indoors. When gadgets have somehow failed to hypnotize some children, it's the academic workload that steps in to curtail their outdoor activities. This situation results in a lopsided equation of input being much more than the output (as shown in the following equation):

Input > output

where, input = number of calories ingested through food
output = number of calories expended through physical exercise

It's evident that in this situation, extra calories enter the body, assuming the form of fat. Ideally, to maintain a good weight, a balance of input and output should be achieved.

So, the ideal equation should be:

Input = output

But if a child is overweight, the energy usage during physical activity (output) has to be more than the calories ingested through food (input) per day.

The equation should then be:

Input < output

At this point, I am tempted to mention that when I was a kid, there were absolutely no distractions in the form of computers, video games, tablets or mobile phones. Even the basic black-and-white TV sets served a limited purpose with their not-so-exciting range of humdrum programmes like *Krishi Darshan* and numerous cheerlessly vapid government documentaries which worked as perfect lullabies to put restless children to sleep.

Whether it was by choice or design, there were only a couple of TV programmes to engage us for a maximum span of one hour a day. Besides, schools were much less ruthless with their homework assignments, which meant that the major part of the evening was spent playing with friends. No one, I repeat, no one had to push or even remind us to step out and play. The mere thought of hopscotch, hide and seek, fire in the mountain and other fun games was enough to lure us out of the house. This is sadly missing from the lifestyle of children today, emerging as the prime cause of childhood obesity.

Let us now run through the list of second-string sinners guilty of tipping the scale in favour of obesity.

Secondary Offenders

Genetics or family history: If obesity runs in the family, especially if both the parents are obese, the likelihood of the child being obese is almost 75 per cent. This plight is universally widespread and thus, not restricted to any one country. Whether you go to a shopping mall or visit a restaurant, it is not a rare sight to spot all members of a single family as obese. The question is, who will bell the cat? To put it simply, who can approach these families and tell them upfront that each of them is a live bomb that needs to be detonated before it's too late to save them from the dire ramifications of being obese.

High-energy snack consumption before or between meals: Consumption of high-fat and high-sugar snacks before or between meals is another major reason for piling up the excess kilos. If you observe eating patterns of the children today, you will notice that they munch all day on unhealthy snacks. They eat constantly between their three main meals (breakfast, lunch and dinner). When they should be consuming fruits or some other healthy snacks like nuts, dried fruits, buttermilk, peanut butter with wholewheat toast, they're mostly seen bingeing on chocolates, cookies, colas, chips, canned juices and other such sinful foods.

I am compelled to share another personal anecdote with you. A couple of years back, I noticed that a friend of mine regularly offered a glass of cola to her chubby ten-year-old before he stepped out to play every day. On witnessing this odd custom a few times, curiosity got the better of me. I threw politeness to the wind and asked her the rationale behind this daily ritual. Pat came the reply from a visibly proud mom, 'This provides my little one with instant energy to play well since it has a high sugar content. Our refrigerator is always well-stocked with colas!' Well, I was too dumbfounded to comment on this immediately. All the brainwashing that had to be done was saved for another day.

The point that I'm trying to make here is that she is definitely not a lone ranger lost in the labyrinth of misinformation. There is a whole section of likeminded parents sharing her belief. Not surprisingly then, children nowadays get about one-third of their daily calories from these high-calorie 'energy-providing' sodas. The dietary preferences of the younger generation today have shifted from fruits, vegetables, whole grains, milk and milk products to calorie-dense, fat-laden, sugar-charged and highly processed foods. While these food items are crammed with empty calories, they're grievously lacking in nutritional value.

It's the parents' duty to supervise their kids' eating habits. I am not saying that one should totally restrict a child's access to her favourite treats, but parents have to teach their kids to indulge in these only occasionally and responsibly.

Eating with the cable guy: Eating absent-mindedly while watching TV is one of the most rampant causes of gaining weight. Many distressed parents report that their children are so obsessed with watching TV that they appear drugged while staring at it. In such a 'spaced-out' state, they obviously would have no idea about what they're really eating and how much food they are stuffing in their gaping-in-awe mouths. They are lost to their immediate surroundings and hence, oblivious to the full-fledged eating experience. They're no longer in sync with their real hunger and this mindless munching more often than not leads to obesity.

Eating mindlessly is one issue, but insisting on having a specific junk food while watching TV is yet another concern. A parent who consults me for her child was facing this issue with her six-year-old. The moment her son would plonk himself in front of the TV to watch his favourite show, he would demand a bag of chips with a glass of cola to go with it. Not complying with this unreasonable demand would mean that all hell would break loose. She found it easier to succumb to his quirky demand rather than deal with the ensuing bedlam. This ritual continued for a couple of years till she decided to seek professional help. The lesson learnt: Don't give in to unhealthy demands of children on a routine basis, because once formed, a bad habit may be very difficult to break. This eating pattern will obviously diminish the child's appetite for the real, healthy foods at mealtimes.

Eating out too often: This trend ranks quite high on the list of offenders leading to obesity. With a number of birthday parties, sleepovers and a whole lot of festive occasions round the year to celebrate, eating out has become more of a routine than a rare treat for kids. Even if there is no occasion, boredom often leads parents to treat eating out as a 'blues buster'. These pleasure trips lead children to gorging on heavy meals with huge portions. This kind of emotional eating is detrimental to the well-being of children.

Eating food too fast too soon: Some children are in the habit of gobbling their food and guzzling their beverages as if someone would snatch away their food. This is a detrimental practice as it leaves no time for the stomach to send a message to the brain that the child is feeling full. By the time the message reaches the brain, the damage is done. The child is crammed with food up to his gullet.

Medical factors: Often, certain medical conditions such as hormonal imbalance and metabolic disorders cause obesity. Certain medications such as steroids could also cause excessive weight gain.

Stockpile of junk: Some families are in the habit of stocking up convenience foods like chips, cookies, ice cream, cakes, bottles of fizzy drinks and other high-calorie snacks as a matter of routine in anticipation of guests' arrival. In some other families, it may be done once in a while in preparation for a celebration at home. Children in such families suffer as they're tempted to consume these foods when hunger strikes.

Psychological Offenders

In some cases, children overeat for emotional reasons, such as, to fight depression, stress or just plain boredom. These children are generally the products of psychological issues such as parental neglect, childhood abuse, low self-esteem and a low body image, to name a few. They may turn to different tools to comfort themselves, food being one of them. In case they're the victims of 'food binge disorder', they tend to form a psychological relationship with food where hunger is not the driving force to binge. Weight gain is inevitable in such cases. A healthy physiological relationship with food exists when mere physical hunger propels children to eat.

Complications of Childhood Obesity

At least 5 in 100 children below the age of twenty are overweight/ obese in the country and the numbers are just shooting northwards. If you don't feel shaken and stirred by nurturing an overweight child yet, the following section on complications of obesity should hopefully give a much needed jolt to make you jump off your easy chair of complacency!

Physical Complications

Type 2 diabetes: This is a metabolic disease which is primarily brought on by obesity and inactivity in children. This disease affects the way the body metabolizes sugar, as a diabetic body does not use insulin properly, causing high blood sugar.

High blood pressure and high cholesterol: Obesity in children can lead to plaque formation in the arteries, leading to the risk of heart ailments early in adulthood.

Liver disease: This is caused by an accumulation of fat in the liver, which could eventually cause inflammation and scarring in the liver. In worst cases, it could lead to liver failure.

Metabolic syndrome: It is a cluster of conditions brought on by obesity that can put your child at risk of developing heart disease, diabetes, or other health problems.

Respiratory problems: Children could suffer from breathing disorders like asthma from being overweight.

Bone and joint problems: This problem occurs due to too much pressure on the knees and ankle joints because of an overweight body. There is also a high risk of osteoporosis and arthritis in adulthood.

Sleep disorders: Obstructive sleep apnoea is a condition in which an overweight child has difficulty breathing while sleeping.

Early puberty and menstruation: Being obese can create hormonal imbalances for your child, leading to earlier-than-normal puberty or menstruation.

Social and Psychological Complications

Low self-esteem: Obese children are generally jeered at by their peers. This may lead to low self-confidence in these children.

Depression: Persistent low self-esteem can lead to general hopelessness because of the social isolation of obese kids. This may push them into a full-fledged depression.

Poor social skills: Because overweight children are an anxious lot and are likely to socially withdraw, this could result in poorer social skills.

Bullied/bullies: Overweight children could face the brunt of being bullied or may themselves turn into dreaded bullies in self-defence.

If you feel that I am spooking you by stating the scary spin-offs of obesity, you are spot on! This simply is a wake-up call for the uninformed and also for the informed-yet-unheeding parents, who still give credence to the moth-eaten wisdom of yore that stuffing kids silly with food is the only genuine sign of parental affection.

Prevention of Obesity

So, who can show the backdoor to your children's obesity? No marks for guessing the right answer. It's obviously 'you' because you're the one they look up to when they're young. You are the mother bird and they are your young fledglings. They wait to be fed by their mother, on whom they impose full trust related to every aspect of life, including food. You set the ball rolling for their healthy adulthood. You, as parents, are responsible for bolstering their foundation for a healthy and disease-free adulthood. Therefore, if the foundation (childhood) itself is fragile because it is based on a worthless diet that is devoid of essential nutrients for growth, how will the entire structure (adulthood) stand the test of time?

I believe, the best way out is to work cohesively as a family to banish obesity from our children's lives. Given below are a few preventive measures that can help you achieve this.

Lead by example: As someone has said, 'Children close their ears to advice but open their eyes to example.' If your children see you exercising regularly and eating a healthy diet, they are more likely to be active and inclined towards eating healthy themselves. A dear friend of mine can never declare her lunch closed without popping a piece of chocolate. Trust her five-year-old sharp-witted little brat to follow suit by mimicking her mother every day. My friend's admonition is countered with a snappy comeback, 'Then why do YOU eat chocolate every day, Mama?' End of the matter. So, the key is to keep the whole-family approach in mind and *practise what you preach*! Parents should lead by example as young kids need positive role models to influence their outlook.

Make exercise and outdoor play a part of the daily routine: Emphasize on the positive aspects of exercising or outdoor play. Plan family activities to make exercise such as running, biking, walking or swimming fun for children. Never make it look like a chore. Our aim should be to get them moving and ensure they get their daily dose of exercise.

Involve children in shopping for healthy fruits and vegetables: When you shop with your kids for food, they become more aware of healthy foods and are more likely to eat the same.

Reduce frequent food jaunts to restaurants: Eat at home more often as most of the menu options in restaurants are high in fat and calories. Treat your family to outside food only occasionally.

Eat at least one meal as a whole family every day: Children observe and mimic their parents more often than not. If they see their parents eating healthy food, they're more likely to follow suit.

Limit the time kids spend on sedentary activities: These may be watching TV, playing video games, 'whatsapping' on a mobile phone and using other gadgets. These make kids indolent and averse to physical activity.

Turn off the TV and other electronic devices during meal times: This will ensure that children eat conscious of their *actual* appetite.

Never use food as a reward or punishment: This will set the stage for food-related power struggles with your children. If you bribe your child with a promise of a chocolate after she polishes off a bowl of dal–rice, the child will always hold you at ransom for the same bribe every time you ask her to finish a dish she doesn't fancy.

Discourage junk-snacking between meals: Discourage children from bingeing on chips, cookies, heavy milkshakes, sweetened beverages, including fruit juices and fizzy drinks before or between meals. These foods and beverages are very high in calories and could kill the child's appetite for healthier foods at main mealtimes. Also, clear the junk pile from your kitchen, as 'out of sight is out of mind'.

Read, educate and play: This may sound like an oddball solution, but it worked well in my house. Ask your kids to gather information about different nutrients found in different fruits, vegetables, cereals and other nutritious food items. Put your heads together, discuss information and compare notes. If you want to add some punch to the practice, you could turn it into a quiz of sorts (say, about vitamins and minerals). It's like hitting two birds with one stone. While you're trying to educate your children about the goodness of foods, your kids think you're playing a fun quiz with them because you don't make it seem like a deliberate tutorial session. Try it! It may just startle you with its success!

Stay fit to be a model parent: If you are fit and healthy, your children will relate more to your efforts to help them lose excess weight. They will feel proud of how good you look and for the compliments you garner. This will motivate them to stay slim and healthy by emulating you. Dr Miriam Stoppard (British doctor, author, television presenter and advice columnist) is spot on when she says, 'Happy healthy parents make happy healthy children.'

Make school meals healthy: Schools have a huge responsibility of providing nutritious meals to children as many schools these days provide two to three meals daily to their day scholars and all meals to the boarders. They should have a dietician on their panel of experts who should plan weekly meals, keeping the nutritious value of each food item in mind.

Whenever parents consult me for their overweight or underweight children, I make it a point to ask them about their schools' weekly menu. It's distressing to find some of the most reputed schools offering doughnuts, greasy pakodas, samosas, bread rolls, French fries and excessively sweetened beverages to their students. It's obvious that parents think educators know their job well and thus, are contented with the schools' food choices. Parents should question the schools about the meal plans, give regular suggestions about adding a nutritious food, or removing a worthless food from the menu and if need be, meet the school's meal planner once in a while.

Many parents who send lunch boxes along with their kids confess to packing junk food like cookies, cakes, fried potato wedges, Maggi noodles, chips, white bread sandwiches with Nutella spread, or too much butter in their kids' tiffin boxes in order to appease them with food of their choice to avoid power struggles. Parents have to remember that they have a responsibility to pack healthy snacks for their kids, as every meal counts towards making them healthy individuals.

The Verdict

It's very evident that lifestyle diseases earlier known only to affect adults, are now brazenly eroding the health fabric of our kids. However, if the parents tightly hold the rein of the health of their kids in their hands and give it a little tug as and when needed, I'm sure children will grow up with a normal body weight and give obesity a big snub!

So, the verdict is loud and clear. Having a fat child is NOT a matter of great pride. We, as parents, need to do a reality check on how we bring up our children. The clock is incessantly ticking. I like what Benjamin Franklin once said, 'You may delay, but time will not.' So act now!

Chapter 12
Help! My Child is All Skin and Bones
Tackling Malnourishment

While the excessive media brouhaha about the detriments of obesity in children continues, there are many parents who find themselves perched on the other side of the spectrum. Their woes are diametrically opposed to the parents of overweight children as they agonize over their kids being skinny and underweight. At their wits' end, they keep the panic button pressed, going to the extent of force-feeding their children mindlessly. Does this do any good? 'If I don't force-feed her, then how will she put on weight and be healthy?' I often get asked this question from the distraught parents of my underweight little clients. So, if you qualify as a paranoid parent of an underweight child, read on!

Before you assume that having an underweight child is a very grave issue, you need to calm down, take a deep breath and understand what being underweight really means and how dire are its consequences.

On the BMI (Body Mass Index) percentile, 5th percentile to 85th percentile, is considered a healthy weight. A child is 'technically' considered underweight if she is below the 5th percentile. After BMI-for-age is calculated for children, this BMI number is plotted on the age-growth chart for children and the percentile ranking is obtained. The percentile indicates the relative position of the child's BMI number among children of the same sex and age. The growth charts show the weight status categories used for children and teens (underweight, healthy weight, overweight and obese).

I had mentioned that below 5th percentile rankers are considered 'technically' underweight. This statement has an implicit connotation. This means that being underweight could be due to any reason, and that the 'technically underweight' child needn't necessarily be an unhealthy child. Let me defog this further. A child may be underweight due to any of the following reasons: genetics; digestive track diseases; low-fat diet; ingestion of very little food due to being a fussy eater; increased metabolic rate due to illnesses like hyperthyroidism; behavioural issues like Attention Deficit Hyperactivity Disorder (ADHD), anorexia nervosa and so on; medical conditions such as protein sensitivity; and certain kinds of medication.

Now, if a child is underweight due to her genetic make-up (that is, if both her parents are very lean), it is normal for the child to be remarkably thin as she would have inherited her thin frame from both her parents. In such cases, where genetics play a role in the child's skinniness, the doctor may not prescribe any specific treatment. Parents in this situation needn't fret if the child is physically and mentally active. She is probably blessed with a very good metabolism and burns calories faster than you could imagine. Most underweight kids put on some weight once their eating habits change as they grow.

If the reasons for being underweight are medical in nature, your physician's intervention is needed at the earliest. However, if the child is underweight due to a low-fat diet or inadequate intake of calories in general due to food aversions, here are a few handy tips to rectify the deficient diet and offset the calorie deficit in a smart way.

Strategies to Nourish a Malnourished Child

Add calorie-dense foods: Feed the child calorie-loaded foods that can give a quick calorie boost to nourish the body. Even two to three spoons of these foods are enough to gratify the little tummy if the child refuses to take in any more food. So, make each bite count. Given below are some ideas for calorie-rich foods:

❏ Full-fat dairy products such as milk, fresh milk cream, cheese, curd, cottage cheese, instead of low-fat dairy products

❏ Peanut butter on toast in place of low-fat spreads

❏ Scrambled eggs on toast with added milk or fresh milk cream rather than plain boiled eggs

❏ Chicken, paneer or cheese sandwich in place of just a vegetable or chutney sandwich

❏ Chicken salad with olive oil dressing instead of plain fresh salad

❏ Dahi chicken (made with full-fat curd and chicken)

❏ Banana, sapota (cheeku) or mango smoothie with nuts like almond and walnuts rather than low-fat apple smoothie without nuts

❏ Avocado paste on toast or guacamole in place of a bread-and-butter combo

❏ Stuffed parantha instead of plain parantha

❏ A heavy and healthy cereal like muesli rather than light and crispy cereals

Some other high-calorie food ideas include cheese balls; boiled and mashed potato with melted cheese on it; boiled sweet potato with a hint of butter; curd rice; fruit yogurt made of full-fat milk; full-fat milk-based puddings like rice kheer, fruit custard, vermicelli kheer or gajar halwa; fruits like banana, mango, litchi, grapes and avocado rather than only low-calorie fruits like apple, orange and guava; banana, cheeku or mango milkshakes; soups with full-fat milk, almond paste or cream in place of water-based clear soups; dried fruits like dates, apricots, plums, figs, raisins and black currant; trail-mix or granola with nuts, seeds, dried fruit or honey; and a handful of nuts like almonds, walnuts, pistachios and cashew nuts.

Warning: Full-fat dairy, including ghee, are high on saturated fats which could be harmful in the long term for heart health. So, exercise restraint wherever possible by resorting to other non-dairy but high-on-calorie foods too.

Add protein: Try feeding your child good sources of protein for adequate tissue and muscle growth. Such food items would include eggs; fish like sardines and salmon ; chicken and poultry; soya products such as soymilk, tofu, soy flour and soybean sprouts; dried beans like chickpeas, black-eyed peas, black chickpeas, kidney beans, navy beans and dried peas; lentils; and quinoa.

Add good fats: These are a source of concentrated energy that can benefit thin and wiry kids. Add:

- ❐ Flaxseed powder to sandwiches, cereals, roti, curries and other food items
- ❐ Olive oil to salads, pasta and noodles
- ❐ Ghee (clarified butter) to rotis and dals
- ❐ Avocado to salads or as a sandwich spread

Pack in some energy-boosters: If some high-nutrition foods cut no ice with your brat and he refuses to eat these as stand-alone foods, beef-up the calories of regular dishes by camouflaging and implanting these power foods in them. Therefore, add:

- ❐ Grated cheese to pulao, vegetables, sandwiches, bakes
- ❐ Grated, mashed or crumbled paneer to curries, pulao, vegetables, sandwiches and bakes
- ❐ Soy granules to curries, pulao, vegetables
- ❐ Shredded and boiled chicken to curries, pulao, vegetables, sandwiches, soups
- ❐ Finely chopped dried fruits to milk drinks, pulao, desserts
- ❐ Grated or powdered nuts to curries, milk drinks, pulao, desserts, soups

❏ Chicken broth to curries and soups
❏ Boiled and minced eggs to sandwiches, pulao, salads
❏ Raw eggs to soups while they're being cooked

Offer six to seven smaller meals: Underweight kids need to eat small and frequent meals rather than three big and phased-out meals. These kids may not get all the energy they need from three meals a day and therefore, would need two to three healthy snacks additionally, to boost their energy intake.

Forbid munching between meals: Discourage munching between scheduled meals. Especially avoid giving juices and high-sugar foods between meals as they can kill the appetite. Your child should be sufficiently hungry at mealtimes to do adequate justice to food.

Curb the craving to drink water during a meal: Dissuade your underweight child from drinking much water just before or during a meal, as even water can fool her into believing that her stomach is full. To make sure the child is not dehydrated, offer water after the meal.

Don't offer junk to make up for the calorie deficit: Offering junk food to your skinny child under the assumption that 'everything that he eats counts towards his growth', does no good to his health. Remember, you don't want him to gain weight at the cost of good nutrition. Underweight children need nutrients like vitamins, minerals, good carbohydrates, good fats and proteins even more than the children of healthier weights. Therefore, shun chips, burgers, cookies, or sodas and offer clean calories to your child.

Silence that sweet craving with healthier options: Here are some healthy ideas for satisfying that sweet craving of your young one: fruit custard; rice or semolina or bulgur wheat kheer; fruit yogurt; dark chocolate-dipped strawberries; frozen chocolate bananas; fruit and yogurt parfait; chocolate popcorn made with peanut butter and dusting of cocoa powder; fruit smoothies; watermelon popsicles; oatmeal-nut apple pie; and grilled apple with cheese and honey.

Warning: Be careful of overindulging your child's sweet tooth with sugar as that can transform a healthy dessert into an unhealthy one. Try adding fruits, dried fruits or a little honey as sweeteners wherever possible to avoid empty sugar calories.

Accelerate the eating process while the child is willing: Fussy eaters are very likely to change their mind from 'yearning to eat' to 'sealing their mouths at the sight of food'. So, always stay in the saddle, combat-ready with the right ammunition in the form of nutritious snacks before your child changes her mind. Keep the following foods ready:

- ❏ Her favourite fruits and vegetables, peeled, sliced or chopped (to be eaten alone or with healthy dips)
- ❏ Healthy dips and spreads like hummus, mint chutney, hung-curd dip, peanut butter (to be eaten with finger foods or as a bread spread)
- ❏ Chicken, shredded and boiled (for chicken sandwich)
- ❏ Eggs, boiled (to be added to sandwich)
- ❏ Cheese, grated (to be sprinkled on any dish)
- ❏ Potatoes, boiled and mashed (as a side dish or added to a sandwich)
- ❏ Cottage cheese, cubed (to be eaten as a snack or added to various dishes)
- ❏ Curd, set at home (needed for fruit yogurt, curd rice, dips and so on)

A caveat: Be careful not to run amuck with my high-calorie suggestions by overdoing them mindlessly. I don't want you to be running amuck the next time, shouting, 'Honey, I blew up the kid!' as I did when I was told my son was obese due to overfeeding.

The Verdict

Sometimes it is possible that an increase in height precedes a gain in weight. In such a scenario, the child may just appear to be underweight for a specific period until his weight gain catches up. In yet another scenario, a child may actually be of a healthy weight, but may appear to be underweight and the odd-one-out, because the rest of his family members may be overweight.

So, prudence says, 'Don't panic'! Be patient and try the above weight-gain tips. Weight gain does take time but it is achievable with diet interventions. If this doesn't work, consult your child's paediatrician.

Chapter 13

Picky Palates

Dealing with the Fussy-eater

What's All the Fuss About?

The other day, a visibly harassed parent of a two-year-old waited to pour her woes out on me the moment she walked in for a diet consultation. As always, I sneaked a quick look at the mom–daughter duo to make a wild guess at the reason for her trepidation. And presto! I was right! The mother was one of the many victims of 'mealtime warfare' that I meet on a regular basis. She recounted her woeful story about the little fussy-eater (visibly embarrassed at the beans being spilled in front of a stranger) sitting quietly with her innocent wide eyes. So here I was, repeating to her what I rattle out to many similarly distressed parents—that she is not the lone victim of this predicament, that the problem is widespread and truly global.

Feeding a fussy-eater is nothing short of a battleground that can stress out parents big time. In short, it's as easy as herding cats! It is partly because of a phenomenon called 'food phobia' which is fairly rampant amongst toddlers and young children. The afflicted ones resist or refuse to eat new foods. This is a normal phase in a child's development and as the kids grow up through adolescence and teenage years, most of them generally grow out of this fix.

In keeping with the spirit of championing the cause of all things nutritious, I have this strong urge to swagger about my imaginary love for fruits, vegetables and all things healthy during my childhood. But woe is me! I wasn't exactly born with the flavour of a carrot or green beans in my mouth, nor did I fall in love with vegetables any time before I learnt to cook (and that was in my mid-twenties). With fruits too, it wasn't exactly love at first bite.

I sniff a sense of déjà vu here. Come on, admit that most of you have been members of 'I-hate-most-things-healthy' club as children. Then, why the hypocrisy now? Why are we so impatient with our kids when they display the same attribute? We panic without realizing that this is but a temporary stage that shall pass.

Top Tips for Dealing with Fussy-eaters

Mealtimes don't necessarily have to be frustrating and exasperating. Consider the following strategies to avoid power struggles and help the picky eater to eat a balanced diet:

Small is big when introducing a new food: Serve a very small portion of the new food so that your child doesn't feel psychologically swamped by the portion. Even two bites of a new food is a positive sign that the child may take well to that food in future attempts. Also, try introducing the new food earlier in the day when your little one is most energetic and least aggressive. This will reduce resistance.

Small is safe: Big portions can overwhelm small children. They may panic looking at the food they're expected to polish off in one go. For instance, if children are sick of regular idlis, cook button-sized ones; if they feel intimidated by the size of a big, square parantha, cook small triangular ones to revive their interest in these foods.

A point to remember is that many kids are genuinely small eaters and feel satiated with comparatively lesser food. So, it's actually sadistic to be satisfied with your parental skills only once you stuff the apple of your eye up to his eyeballs.

Small bites, big calories: Make each calorie count as it's advisable to feed children calorie-rich healthy foods every three hours or so. Even two to three spoons full of high-calorie but healthy foods are enough at one go for the little tummies. (Refer to Chapter 12, 'Help! My Child is all Skin and Bones' for calorie-dense food ideas).

Serve the new with the old: Don't take your culinary skills for granted with your fussy little eater. Always have your back-up plan ready by serving a familiar food that your child can eat without a fuss, along with the new food. And just in case your new food plan falls apart and your baby refuses to even sniff it, neither force her to eat it, nor give up trying totally. Keep offering the food to her from time to time since children's taste buds constantly change.

A big 'NO' to pleading, pestering and forcing: If your little one refuses food, do not, I repeat, DO NOT coax her to eat. If you fuss regularly and implore her to eat unwillingly, she is likely to start associating mealtimes with anxiety and frustration.

I have been a witness to my niece's ordeal when my cousin would immobilize her by pinning her down and then force food spoon after spoon through her firmly pursed lips. The little one would howl, plead, cough, hold her breath and still worse, look at me through her tear-filled eyes imploring me to save her from the perpetrator. For the hapless little child, mealtimes turned into a battlefield! This was too heartrending a sight to witness and a totally avoidable one.

The fallout in her case: she remained a fervid food-hater for many years to come. So, it's crystal clear that force-feeding on a regular basis is counter-productive. You don't want your child to dislike food, do you? That certainly doesn't augur well for you. Please remember that hunger is a primary requirement of the body and a child will not remain hungry for long. She will herself ask for food when hunger comes a-calling.

Shun bribing: Bribing kids or offering them food rewards on the condition of cleaning up a platter of healthy food could lead to negative associations with foods in question. Conditional acquisition of their favourite food can turn the little ones into manipulative goblins. Every time you want your child to eat a healthy food that he so vehemently refuses, you would have to promise him an unhealthy treat. Can you imagine how much junk you would feed him in this way? Instead, give your child non-food rewards. These could be tokens, coins, stickers, or even extra play time in the park.

Be a positive role model: Children like to mimic parents. So, if you'd like your child to eat a particular food, you too should eat it in her presence. Put up a healthy-food-eating-act if you have to. For instance, eat a fruit or a breakfast cereal with so much zest that your child gets a feeling that you just love eating it. She is likely to follow suit, moved by the little theatrics that you put up in her honour. This could go a long way in helping your child form a healthy eating habit.

Family meals work wonders: Eat at least one meal as a family. Kids are more likely to eat the foods they don't fancy if the whole family is eating the same food together. When the family sits together, chats and laughs together, the atmosphere is relaxed and stress-free. It is easier to expect your child to have a more positive outlook towards food than when she is being fed alone and knows that all the focus is on her.

Flee from the fillers: Avoid filling up your child on sweetened beverages and junk snacks for most part of the day as it might decrease her appetite for the main meals. Snacks like juices, chocolates, chips and cookies generally fill kids' little tummies, leading them to fuss or refuse main meals.

Bank on creativity: Creativity seldom hurts! Use your ingenuity to dish out imaginative and appealing food. Ideas are aplenty. Some handy pointers for you are listed below:

❐ Cut foods into various shapes. Use different shaped cookie cutters and moulds to cut and bake food. Children generally love food in offbeat shapes like a watermelon cut into a star shape or a grape and a cheese cube on a toothpick.

❐ Use a variety of brightly coloured foods, or add colourful vegetable puree or pieces to foods like roti, idli, uttapam, curd or smoothies.

❐ Tell stories about the food—for instance, help your kid's imagination to take a flight of fancy by asking her to imagine each bite to be an aircraft landing at the airport, which is her mouth.

❐ You could manipulate your child's favourite TV characters in your favour. My son was a crazy fan of Popeye and Bugs Bunny. So, it was a cakewalk for me to feed him spinach and carrots. He loves them to date.

❐ Assign dishes playful names. Use names such as 'idli buttons', 'apple moons', 'banana wheels', 'pea balls', 'egg boats', 'cheese snowballs', 'parantha stars' and so on.

❐ Experiment with textures, as sometimes it's the texture that doesn't go well with kids' taste buds. For example, if your child refuses to eat soft or pureed foods such as bananas or yogurt, try offering crunchy foods like carrots or apples. If your child is bored with pureed, mashed, or curried dishes, offer finger foods. If she hates pineapples, offer her diced pineapple with diced cheese on a toothpick and so on.

❐ Use attractive and vibrant crockery like bowls, plates and spoons with favourite cartoon characters, favourite colours, whacky shapes, miniature toy sets—let your imagination flow.

Old food in the garb of new: If your child suddenly decides to veto the foods that he ate happily till now, it's time to reinvent them. For instance, if he refuses to eat dal–palak, try a cheese–spinach bake; instead of carrot–aloo subzi, serve raw carrot with a healthy dip; if he shuns eggs with sunny-side up, offer him scrambled eggs or a boiled egg-cheese sandwich. So, change the way you cook the food that has lost favour with him and see him fill his plate with it again.

Raw can be a big draw: Many a times, vegetables may appeal to children in their raw form rather than their cooked version. Enhance their appeal by offering them with some healthy dips such as hummus or dill and a hung curd dip; or in a salad form with a healthy salad dressing like sesame vinaigrette dressing, green goddess dressing and so on.

A little gimmick (offered with good intent) won't hurt: If your child feels overwhelmed by the portions served to her, trick her by serving a regular meal portion in an adult-size dinner plate. This will make her meal appear really small and she is more likely to bite the bait without much ado.

Don't kowtow to 'Hunger Games': Avoid preparing a fresh meal for your child after he rejects the planned meal. This is sure to promote picky eating as kids are smart enough to understand that they can get away easily by creating a fuss around food. Most mothers tend to panic if the food is completely rejected by the child. They would imagine their little ones to be pitifully hungry and their hearts would go out to them. Mothers would willingly go through the rigours of cooking their kids' preferred meals afresh lest they're held guilty (by their own conscience) for starving their kids. These are the games children play. Just wrap up the meal and stash it away for later when the child feels really hungry. After a few such instances, watch them eat what was served to them earlier. They will know that their emotional blackmail has stopped working on their recently turned-wiser mothers.

Colour them bright: Always keep a variety of healthy foods like fruits and vegetables with different colours in attractive trays or bowls within reach of children. Your fussy-eater may just surprise you one day by choosing a fruit she generally refuses to eat. Hunger pangs can sometimes change the relationship kids have with certain foods.

A little drama doesn't hurt either: Make positive comments about the food you are eating, such as 'This is yummy!' This may make the child curious enough to try it.

Praise them aplenty: Laud your child when he surprises you by eating without a fuss, because toddlers respond well to positive strokes. Be sure to commend him even if he tries only a couple of bites and then refuses to cover any more ground. Your praise will ensure that they keep gratifying you by trying the same food again after a little gap. Soon, eating that healthy food just to solicit your lavish praise will become a habit with him.

Grant some control to the kid: Allow your baby to touch her food and play with it if she wants to. This may change the status of this food from strange to familiar in her mind. Let her even mess around if she so desires. This will teach her to eat her meals independently. In the bargain, there may be spilt food, sticky floor, soiled clothes and a lot more mess you didn't bargain for. But it's a small price to pay for teaching your child to eat on her own without a fuss. Also, don't hang about constantly. This makes the child conscious of your continual hawk-like supervision. This in turn leads to a stressful situation for the child and takes away a lot of pleasure of experimenting with food.

Don't panic, stay calm: Don't get worried and feel guilty if one meal turns into a disaster. The world is not coming crashing down on you. This is a normal phenomenon. Put the episode behind you and approach the next meal with immense positivity. You and your toddler are both on a learning curve. Your toddler is learning to try new flavours and textures and you are learning to cope with tricky mealtimes. Remember, kids cannot and will not remain hungry for long. Even if she tries two bites, you should breathe easy.

Involve your child in the whole process: Take your child shopping for vegetables and fruits and ask him to assist in washing, chopping, stirring and so on in the kitchen. When the kids are roped into this activity, they may feel a sense of importance and inclusion. Thus, they may relate better to the food being cooked with their help.

Educate your child: Teach the children from time to time about the health benefits of healthy food items they dislike. Use props like glossy books and fascinating charts with colourful food pictures to explain. While showing pictures of healthy foods such as fruits, get your baby to touch the actual fruit and maybe taste it too. Take slightly older children to buy fruits and vegetables with you once in a while. Point out different coloured fruits and vegetables to them with their nutrients. For instance, talk about tomatoes, apricots and watermelon sharing the nutrient 'lycopene' that helps prevent the risk of many diseases. Talk about carrots being rich in vitamin A, which is crucial for good eyesight.

While correlation and association of things work wonderfully well with little kids, reiteration will bolster positive images of these foods in your child's mind and may change his perception of food completely.

Build appetite through exercise: Ensure that your little one gets plenty of exercise. That will whet your child's appetite for her meals. She is more likely to approach mealtimes positively when she is really hungry after exercise.

Try until you succeed: Don't give up trying. Studies suggest that it may take ten to fifteen or more exposures to a new food before the child accepts it. It's not unusual for the child to develop an affinity to a previously 'peculiar-tasting' food. You just need to keep the effort on. Remember, it's the child's palate you're training, so expect the ride to be a little choppy!

Disguise food! If your fussy little one refuses even to touch certain foods that are loaded with nutrients, don't lose your sleep over it. Just camouflage these foods cleverly. Listed below are a few smart camouflaging instances:

❐ If your child refuses to eat certain vegetables, sneak them into his parantha/roti/dal/soup/curries/bakes/idlis, in pureed form. Chop/grate them finely and add them to his upma/poha/chilla/idli/uttapam.
❐ If it is milk that has lost favour with him, add it to white sauce in pasta, or serve it through fruit smoothies.
❐ Add boiled and mashed vegetables like carrots, spinach, pumpkin, bottle gourd with mashed potatoes.
❐ Add rejected fruits to smoothies and custard.

Ditch the distractions: Eating a new food while watching TV or while playing with any other gadget, nixes the chances of establishing any connection that your child could have formed with this food. Their little minds are so deeply fixated on the TV that they seldom know what they're being fed. So, the association with the new food is sacrificed because the little brain is overstimulated by what is running on the TV. Children need to focus mainly on food during mealtimes to be able to appreciate what they are putting in their mouth.

Organize a fiesta of good eaters: Once in a while, invite your child's friends who are good eaters to join her for a meal. Watching her friends eat well could really turn things around for you in the fussy-eating department through positive peer pressure.

Give conditional choices: A child feels important and somewhat empowered when you ask her what she wants to eat for dinner. But be smart and give her just a conditional choice. This means that instead of asking her an open-ended question like 'What would you like to eat?', ask her 'Would you like to eat peas or squash?' When you ask an open-ended question, she will name a favourite food more often than not. However, if you give her a choice between two healthy foods, you have a win-win situation.

The Verdict

Remember that your child's eating habits are not likely to change overnight, but they are constantly changing. The small steps you take each day can help promote a lifetime of healthy eating. Your persistence and patience are bound to pay-off sooner than you may believe!

Chapter 14

Snack Attack

Healthy Nibbles for Different Occasions

I vividly remember my childhood days when every evening we salivated and slobbered over the thought of hot, fresh goodies, wondering what the surprise of the day would be. The evening snack was my favourite meal and the wait for this daily ritual was often agonizing. So, I wouldn't be too wrong in assuming that snacking is an important leisure activity for many kids even today. However, it's not as if kids, especially the younger ones, can wolf down big portions at a time. They have small stomachs that cannot handle huge meals at one go. Yet, they need enough calories every day to provide fuel for their activities, build new tissue and sustain growth. So, here's where healthy snacking fits in.

Healthy snacks provide that extra energy to fuel the growing body and bridges nutrient gaps if any. Besides three main meals, most children need two to three smaller snack meals every day. Children generally feel full very quickly at a mealtime, but get hungry just as quickly, which can leave them cranky. A timely snack can balance out these hunger spikes and re-energize little bodies with nutrition.

Healthy Snacking Guidelines

For snacking to be labelled beneficial for your child, there are certain guidelines you need to follow:

❏ The snacks should be healthy and therefore, should be made of one or more nutrients like complex carbohydrates, proteins, good fats, vitamins and minerals.

❏ They should ideally be low in sugar, salt, saturated fats and trans fats.

❏ The snacks should be well timed. They should not be offered close to a main meal so that children are hungry enough for the next meal and more willing to try new foods then.

❏ The times for a snack could be mid-day and after school to help children stay focused on homework and give them enough energy for their evening play or other commitments.

❏ Snacks should be smaller in portion sizes than the main meals, as these are not meal replacement options.

❏ Kids should be given around two to three snacks in a day and not allowed to munch and nibble the whole day. If they do, they can easily lose track of how much they are eating in proportion to their hunger.

❏ Try serving snacks at the same time each day. Structured mealtimes will get them into a healthy habit of expecting snacks only at fixed times instead of 'any-time bingeing'.

❏ Set the stage for healthy snacking by leaving healthy foods like fruits, yogurt, salads and nuts in the fridge and on your child's study table. These will draw her attention and are likely to be picked over food that is out of sight.

❏ Be the role model by making healthy snacking a family habit, as children learn quickly by emulating adults.

Having endorsed the relevance of healthy snacks for children, it's time for me to now classify and review the various categories of snacks, as there are countless options to hone your culinary skills.

Snack Categories

Age-wise 'At Home' and Tiffin Snacks

Toddlers (1–3 years)

Toddlers of this age need around three snacks, apart from the three main meals. Some snack options to fill baby tummies are:

- ❑ semi-boiled carrots, beans, capsicum, cauliflower, zucchini, with a healthy dip like yogurt or hummus.
- ❑ Fruit slices or cubes (big and soft so as not to choke them) like apples, pears and bananas.
- ❑ Peanut butter on wholewheat crackers, wholewheat bread slices, bananas or apple slices.
- ❑ Cereal mix with cornflakes, puffed rice, roughly crushed peanuts and popcorn.
- ❑ Sooji-toast made of wholewheat bread, semolina and a little malai (fresh cream).
- ❑ Stuffed parantha triangles (spinach, methi, carrot, chana dal or beetroot).
- ❑ Banana or carrot bread (homemade).
- ❑ Wholewheat bite-sized pizza with vegetable topping.
- ❑ Pasta with white or marinara sauce.
- ❑ Yellow moong dal or besan chillas (pancakes).
- ❑ Whole grain cereals like wheat flakes and oatmeal.
- ❑ Cheese on wholewheat crackers.
- ❑ Pita chips with hummus (homemade).
- ❑ Cheese cubes, slices or wedges.

Other options include lightly sweetened lassi; banana smoothie; fruit yogurt; rice idlis; uttapam; soft dosa; sooji (semolina) upma; boiled or scrambled egg; cottage cheese cubes; dhoklas; sooji–curd idlis; and cucumber slices.

Pre-schooler (3–5 years)

Pre-schoolers too, need two to three snacks besides the three main meals. Here are some ideas:

- ❑ All items from the toddlers' section.
- ❑ Dried fruits like raisins, plums, fig, dates, peaches and sultanas.
- ❑ A variety of sandwiches with cheese, mint chutney, vegetable or chicken fillings.

❏ Boiled corn with a trace of butter or cheese.

❏ Small pita, roti wraps or kathi rolls with vegetables, paneer, eggs or chicken fillings.

❏ Yellow moong dal, green whole moong dal, besan or sooji chillas.

❏ Puffed rice mixture, which is made with light seasoning, with cornflakes, chana and peanuts added to it.

❏ Mini-pizza made of a wholewheat bread base with a topping made of vegetables of your choice.

Other options include fruit smoothies with nuts; milkshakes; air-popped popcorn; baked soya granule cutlets; poha with potato and peanuts; sooji and vermicelli upma; and sooji–curd idli.

School-going Kids/Teenagers (6–18 years)

Older children need generally two snack meals, one as a mid-day break and one after school or college to revitalize them. Such meals could include:

❏ Raw carrots, capsicum, cauliflower or cucumber with a healthy dip like yogurt dip, low-fat ranch dip, hummus or guacamole.

❏ Fruit smoothies made of low-fat milk or yogurt with nuts and flaxseeds.

❏ Peanut butter on wholewheat toast, sliced banana or apple.

❏ Dosa with or without a vegetable filling.

❏ Wholewheat pizza with vegetables, roasted chicken topping.

❏ Plain or stuffed parantha (with spinach, methi, carrot, chana dal, beetroot, radish or cauliflower) made in minimal oil on a non-stick tawa.

❏ Boiled egg, omelette or scrambled eggs.

❏ Sooji or wholewheat bread toast, with a chopped onion, tomato and a dash of malai (fresh cream).

❏ Yellow moong dal, green whole moong dal, besan or sooji chillas.

❏ Kathi rolls (multigrain flour) with vegetable, egg, chicken or paneer fillings.

❏ Sandwiches (with mint chutney, cheese, boiled chicken or low fat paneer).

❏ Homemade low sugar granola bars (oats, honey, nuts or dried fruits).

❏ Fruit milkshakes with or without a little sugar or honey.

❏ Low-sugar whole grain cereals with low fat milk.

Other excellent options are lightly sweetened lassi; low-sugar or no-sugar fruit yogurt; whole fruit; buttermilk; rice idlis; sooji–curd idli; uttapam; sooji and vermicelli upma; poha with vegetables and/or peanuts; whole grain pita bread with hummus; wholewheat pasta with red sauce; wholewheat pasta salad; dried fruits and nuts; trail-mix with dried fruits, nuts and seeds; corn on the cob; boiled corn; Greek yogurt; sprouts and fruit salad; wholewheat pasta chaat; boiled kabuli chana chaat; and fruit chaat.

On the Move

Whether it's a vacation or a day-trip, you as a parent have the onus of putting together an assortment of snacks that are savoury, yet not 'empty-calorie-fat-laden' goodies. Beware! Your 'super-charged little monsters' will be keeping a lookout for the lard-laden, blubber-making, nutrient-less cookies, candies, waffles, or potato chips, as they have been conditioned to think of these foods as yummy and toothsome.

Most snacking on the go always mean chomping cookies, cakes and candies? The answer is a vehement 'NO'! The expressions 'healthy-eating' and 'fun-eating' can definitely be synonymous with each other. Here is a list of delectable yet healthy and homemade snacks right out of my son's list of favourites:

❑ No-cook granola bars made of jiggery or honey, cinnamon, oats, puffed rice, wheat flakes, almonds, raisins and very little butter.

❑ Fruit chaat made of different coloured fruits such as red and green apples, red and green grapes, strawberries, pomegranates, cherries, kiwis and oranges.

❑ Trail-mix made of puffed rice or wheat flakes, chana with shells, peanuts, pumpkin and sunflower seeds, some dried apricots, raisins, almonds, cashews or walnuts.

❑ Chopped raw vegetables like carrots, radish, cauliflower florets and cucumber served with low-fat dips such as yogurt, bean curd or hummus.

❑ Wholewheat multigrain toast or whole grain crackers with peanut butter spread.

❑ Single-serve cartons of plain, sugarless or low sugar fruit yogurt.

❑ Low-fat bhelpuri made with green mint–coriander chutney, saunth chutney, puffed rice, roasted peanuts, cornflakes, boiled potato, chopped onion and tomato.

❑ Vegetable sandwiches with a variety of fillings like:

- Yogurt herb spread (yogurt + fresh mint+ parsley + minced garlic + salt)
- Cheese and lettuce filling
- Carrot and green peas spread (boiled and chopped carrots + boiled peas + grated low fat paneer to bind + a little flavoured cheese spread + salt + pepper)
- Mint chutney and cheese slice filling

Other favourites are pineapple cheese sticks; chana dal, moong dal or besan chillas; mini sooji–curd idlis; dried cereals with added dried fruits or muesli; and dried fruit like raisins, apricots, dates, prunes and pineapple.

For the Sporty Ones

For the children who are into intense sports or play for extended hours, the diet has to be the right combination of both simple and complex carbohydrates to provide fuel for the body and enough proteins for tissue repair and overall growth. Therefore their diet plan has to include:

- ❏ Proteins like boiled eggs, chicken or egg sandwich, peanut butter on toast.
- ❏ Complex carbohydrates like a wholewheat egg sandwich, wholewheat veggie and cheese sandwich, dried fruits, homemade granola bars or energy bars, banana, boiled sweet potato, pasta in red sauce, parboiled vegetable fingers (carrot, green beans, baby corn, broccoli) with dips, corn on the cob, poha, upma, idli.
- ❏ Simple carbohydrates like lightly sweetened sports drink or lemonade.
- ❏ Good fats like nuts and trail-mix.
- ❏ Dairy-based snacks like fruit milkshakes, fruit yogurt, cheese slices.
- ❏ Legumes, lentils or dried beans like chickpeas salad, hummus, sprouts chaat or salad, three-bean salad or roasted beans.

Season-wise

Summer Savouries

The Indian summer can be very harsh and unsparing for all, especially for our young ones. The sweltering heat and irksome sweat can bother them immensely. While the summer cannot be wished away before it has asserted itself, we can at least make young lives easier. Offer them foods that are light on their tiny tummies have a cooling effect on the body and keep kids energized in this sapping weather. Foods that are acclaimed for alleviating summer stress are:

Fruits: While all fruits provide energy, fruits that pack a punch in beating the heat are:

❏ Watermelon: It is the best thirst quencher and acts as a coolant for the body with a water content of 92 per cent.

❏ Cantaloupe: This juicy and pulpy fruit is ideal for summer. It helps maintain the electrolyte balance in the body.

❏ Grapes: They increase the blood volume in the body, banishing weakness that is caused by heat.

❏ Sweet lime: This citrus and juicy fruit peps up the energy levels.

❏ Mango: An undisputed favourite, it brims with natural sugars and hence is a great source of energy.

❏ Orange: A major thirst-quencher, this juicy fruit is a great energy-booster for the little ones who need to refuel themselves after physical activity every day.

❏ Coconut flesh: Is a great energy-booster and is very good for the skin, especially during the harsh Indian summer.

Vegetables: Light to digest, water-based vegetables are recommended for the summer. Some vegetable-based snacks are:

❏ Tomato–cucumber–lettuce salad: While tomatoes are easy on the stomach during the sapping summers by virtue of their juiciness, cucumbers and lettuce keep the body cool because of their water content.

❏ Cucumber–tomato–cheese sandwich: It makes for a wholesome carbs and protein snack.

Beverages: These would include:

❏ Aam panna (made of raw mangoes): This lip-smacking drink is a preventive recipe for heat stroke. It also prevents the loss of excessive sodium chloride and iron from the body that occurs due to profuse sweating.

- ❑ Wood apple (bel) juice: Wood apple fruit is a coolant that is used to treat heat stroke.
- ❑ Buttermilk (chhach): It is an excellent source of probiotics and has a cooling effect on the body.
- ❑ Lassi/curd: Yogurt has the same cooling effect on the body as buttermilk.
- ❑ Coconut water: This is nature's most refreshing drink and a great electrolyte replacement.
- ❑ Fruit smoothies: Both fruits and yogurt have a cooling effect on the body, so their combination in a smoothie helps fight summer heat effectively.
- ❑ Cold soups: They provide a nutritious base for a meal without adding heat to the body and are light on the stomach.

Winter Windfall

What's better than savoury delights on a nippy winter day to warm your little ones up?

Fruits: Winter brings with it a bagful of fruity delights. Pamper your child with a whole array of fruits. This list has been handpicked by my son in order of his preferences and therefore, has the endorsement of a child: banana; kiwi; guava; pineapple; pomegranate; pear; cheeku; and apple.

Vegetables: While children may fuss about the lack of adequate food choices during summer, the winter season offers a wide, vibrant range of vegetable-based snacks such as:

- ❑ Sweet potato: It is a delicious snack that provides ample energy. Give a boiled sweet potato with a pinch of salt and a dash of lemon to your kid instead of cookies.
- ❑ Carrot: Remember Bugs Bunny with his signature carrot? My son drew inspiration from the iconic cartoon to eat this scrumptious vegetable and loves it to date.

❐ Fresh green garbanzos: Fresh green chickpeas taste wonderful. Eat them raw or boil them, add some tomatoes, onions, salt, lemon juice and red chilli powder and serve as a healthy snack to your little ones.

Dried fruits and nuts: Dried fruit and nuts make for a delicious snack between meals for the kids. You could even sneak in a handful of these in your kid's tiffin box. Nuts that are great in the Indian winter are almonds, walnuts, pistachios and peanuts. Some dried fruits you could dip into are raisins, apricots, dates, plums and figs.

Dried fruits and nuts will not only keep your kids warm but will also satisfy their sweet cravings in a healthy way.

Hot soups: A bowl of hot soup on a cold winter evening is nutritious and gives warmth. Remember, packaged soups are avoidable. Some of the healthy winter soup options, among many others, are tomato, vegetable , tomato–spinach, carrot–bean, clear chicken noodle, butternut or wild mushroom soup. Tomato shorba and tomato rasam are other delicious options.

Snacking During Study Time

Exam time stress is known to cause nervous exhaustion and in extreme cases, emotional collapse. Although there are a number of interventions needed to alleviate exam stress like proper sleep, meditation, deep breathing, proper hydration or listening to soothing music, a nutritious diet also plays a significant role in easing out stress, improving performance and sharpening focus and concentration.

These are some of the snacks that are likely to help during study prep: hot chocolate; fruits like bananas, berries, avocados; trail-mix with seeds, dried fruits and nuts; seeds like pumpkin, sunflower and flaxseed; nuts like walnuts, almonds and hazelnuts; and vegetables like boiled white potato, boiled sweet potato, boiled broccoli and cauliflower with low-fat dips.

Other enticing options are tomato salad; vegetable juice; dried fruits; sprouted grain salad; air-popped popcorn; wholewheat multigrain bread; eggs; and cereal with milk.

Weight-wise

Obese or Overweight

The parents of overweight kids need to watch the calories their children ingest each day. They also need to trim away empty calories added through simple carbohydrates and fatty foods. Here are some snack options:

❏ Semi-boiled carrots, beans, capsicum, cauliflower, zucchini, with a healthy dip like yogurt or hummus.
❏ Fruit yogurt made of skimmed milk without added sugar.
❏ Whole fruits like apples, pears, bananas, papayas, guavas, oranges, sweet lime, kiwi, cherries and berries.
❏ Cereal mix with cornflakes, puffed rice and chana with shells.
❏ Low-sugar, whole grain cereals with low fat milk.
❏ Homemade bhelpuri with mint chutney, boiled potato, with sev puri and with little or no sweet chutney.
❏ Stuffed small roti (spinach, methi, carrot, chana dal or beetroot).
❏ Fruit smoothie with low-fat milk or yogurt.
❏ Wholewheat bread sandwiches with mint chutney and vegetables.
❏ Yellow moong dal, green whole moong dal or besan chillas.
❏ Wholewheat crackers without cheese.

Other options are sooji–curd or rice idlis, uttapam, plain dosa, upma, poha, boiled eggs, wholewheat pita chips with low-fat hummus, wholewheat pasta salad, air-popped popcorn with a trace of salt, buttermilk, corn on the cob, boiled corn, sprout salad, wholewheat pasta chaat, boiled kabuli chana chaat, dried peas chaat and fruit chaat.

Malnourished/Underweight

Here are some snack options for kids who are underweight:

- ❏ Sweet lassi made of full-fat milk yogurt.
- ❏ Banana smoothie made with full-fat yogurt with added nuts.
- ❏ Fruits like mangoes, cheekus, litchis, bananas, grapes, pineapples and custard apples.
- ❏ Peanut butter on wholewheat crackers, wholewheat bread slices, banana or apple slices.
- ❏ Wholewheat pizza with paneer or chicken topping.
- ❏ Stuffed parantha (spinach, methi, carrot, chana dal, beetroot, potato or paneer) with minimal oil.
- ❏ Dried fruits like raisins, plums, fig, dates, peaches, sultanas.
- ❏ Homemade granola bars (oats, honey, nuts, dried fruits, seeds).
- ❏ Sooji or wholewheat bread toast, with a little fresh cream.

Other snacks that they can tuck into are cheese cubes, slices or wedges; cheese on wholewheat crackers; aloo masala dosa; scrambled eggs with full-fat milk; paneer cubes from full-fat milk; sandwiches with chicken or cheese; milkshakes from full-fat or toned milk; kathi rolls with vegetables, paneer, chicken or egg filling; and boiled corn with cheese.

Some Innovative Snack Options

Snacks can be as creative as you'd like them to be and some great ideas (courtesy the blog: 'Foodfellas 4 You') are watermelon pizza; vada pau sandwiches; no-bake, no-fry pinwheels; vadas (almost oil-free) in appe pan; warm brussels sprouts salad with balsamic glaze; dalia idlis; buckwheat idlis; buckwheat dosa; multigrain dalia dosa; kala chana bhel; moong dal bhel; grilled sprouts sandwiches; avocado thepla or khakra; guacamole on tomato slices; no-fry dahi pakodi in appe pan; cucumber avocado dip; black chana hummus; BBQ shakarkandi and pineapple chaat; no-fry dahi vadas filled with sprouts salad; and quinoa–brussels sprouts salad.

Note: Wherever possible, you can make every snack healthier by the following swaps:

- ❏ Multigrain flour instead of refined flour or plain flour.
- ❏ Wholewheat bread instead of white bread.
- ❏ Boiled potatoes in place of fried potato filling.
- ❏ Minimal oil spray in non-stick pan instead of regular frying.
- ❏ A little honey instead of sugar.
- ❏ Cook in air-fryer or steam in appe pan instead of deep-frying fritters or vadas.

The Verdict

Training your children to snack healthy is definitely not a cakewalk—it's a journey fraught with a zillion tantrums and ample hysterics. But you cannot give up! As a conscientious parent, you need to condition your child to make healthy snack choices which will build the base for a lifetime of healthy eating. Nutritious snack ideas are plentiful. So, what are you waiting for? Start experimenting or scout for healthy recipes now! You never know when your little one's hunger pangs may come a-calling!

Chapter 15

Bite Me, I'm Bliss!

Toothsome and Healthy Recipes

Who says healthy and tasty are antonyms of each other and cannot describe the same food? Should all that is nutritious always imply unsavoury and humdrum fare? Hell no! It's a big fat fallacy which needs to be challenged assertively for the sake of our younger generation's health. The onus lies on us, the parents, who need to put the fun and taste back into our children's healthy meals. It is not as much hard work as some of us think. With a little planning and advance preparation, we can transform the dining area from a battleground to a peaceful and sought-after dining room during mealtimes.

I have put up an assortment of healthy, innovative, yet simple meals and snacks, sourced straight from the kitchens of some creative mums that I have the good fortune of knowing.

Munch-Time Treats

Kidney Bean Fritters

Ingredients

1 cup cooked quinoa
1 cup boiled red kidney beans
¼ cup brown bread crumbs
1 cup mixed vegetables, finely chopped (onion, peppers, zucchini and mushrooms)
¼ cup spring onions, chopped
Ginger, garlic and green chilli, to taste
Salt, red chilli and black pepper powder, to taste
Greek yogurt

Water, as needed
Mint chutney

Method

Mash red kidney beans and then mix all the other ingredients with water.

Form fritters in circles using a cookie cutter to maintain consistency.

Heat up the grill pan and grill the fritters evenly.

Serve with Greek yogurt and mint chutney.

(Courtesy: Adya Shukla, Healthy Cooking Contest,
Food Stalking Group on Facebook)

Corn and Potato Tikkis

Ingredients

¾ cup sweet corn kernels, boiled and coarsely crushed
1½ cups potatoes, boiled, peeled and mashed
2 tbsp coriander (dhania), finely chopped
2 tsp lemon juice
2 tsp green chillies, finely chopped
½ tsp garam masala
8 low fat cheese slices made into balls
Oil (canola/olive) for greasing/shallow frying in non-stick pan
Salt to taste

Method

Combine corn, potatoes, coriander, lemon juice, green chillies, garam masala and salt in a deep bowl and mix well.

Divide the mixture into 8 equal portions and shape each portion into a small round each.

Press a little in the centre of each round to make a depression, place a cheese ball in each depression and again shape them back into round balls. Flatten them lightly between your palms to make a small tikkis.

Brush oil on a heated non-stick tava, place the tikkis on it and cook on medium flame till they are golden brown in colour on both sides.

Serve immediately with green chutney.

Note: Tikkis can be made even healthier by steaming them in a pan with oil just to grease the grooves of the pan.

(Courtesy: Anuradha Gaikwad, Healthy Cooking Contest,
Food Stalking Group on Facebook)

Crispy Triangles

Ingredients

½ cup sooji (semolina)
4 tsp curd
2 wholewheat/multigrain bread slices
⅓ cup carrot, grated
⅓ cup capsicum, finely chopped
A handful of coriander leaves, chopped
½ tsp flaxseeds
Salt and pepper to taste

Method

Mix sooji with 3–4 tsp curd. Add carrot, capsicum, coriander, flaxseeds, salt and pepper. Keep aside.

Cut the bread slices into 2 triangles each.

With a blunt knife, layer the bread slice with this mixture.

On a hot non-stick tawa, spray a little olive oil, let it heat. Add a triangle with the pasty side down. Reduce the flame. Keep pressing lightly for 1–2 minutes and then flip it on the other side. Serve hot with green chutney.

(Courtesy: Rashmi Sanghi, Healthy Cooking Contest,
Food Stalking Group on Facebook)

Soft Ragi Idli (Plain or Stuffed)

Ingredients

¾ cup urad dal
¼ cup rice
1½ cup ragi flour

½ tsp flaxseed powder
½ tsp baking soda/Eno salt
Mixed vegetables (cabbage, capsicum, carrot and beans), grated or finely chopped
A pinch of salt
Water

Method

Soak dal and rice for 4–6 hours.

Blend both dal and rice separately in the blender.

Add ragi flour to this ground dal and rice mixture. Add salt and mix well. Cover and let it ferment overnight.

After fermentation, add baking soda and flaxseed powder. Mix well again.

Grease the moulds and put batter in the moulds. Add vegetables and cover them with some more batter on top of them.

Steam idlis till cooked properly.

Serve with mint chutney.

(Courtesy: Anamika Khippal, Healthy Cooking Contest,
Food Stalking Group on Facebook)

Paddu

Ingredients

3 cups of rice
1 cup urad dal
1 big onion, chopped
2 carrots, chopped
1 capsicum, chopped
½ cup parboiled peas
½ cup green beans
A handful of coriander, chopped
Green chillies to taste
Salt to taste

Method

Soak rice and dal overnight.

Finely ground both rice and dal to a paste.

Add all the vegetables to the batter.

Fill the grooves of a paddu pan/appam pan with the batter. Cover the top. Steam them for 5–6 minutes.

Serve hot with mint or tomato chutney.

(Courtesy: Gowri Ravi, Healthy Cooking Contest,
Food Stalking Group on Facebook)

Sweet Corn Beany Salad

Ingredients

3 cups kidney beans, boiled and cooled
1 cup sweet corn, boiled and cooled
1 cup paneer, crushed
¾ cup capsicum, diced
1 tbsp lemon juice
1 tsp Italian seasoning
Salt and pepper to taste

Method

Mix all the above and chill in the refrigerator before serving.

(Courtesy: Hena Gupta, Healthy Cooking Contest,
Food Stalking Group on Facebook)

Egg Salad

Ingredients

2 boiled eggs
2 stalks of celery, finely chopped
1 small onion, finely chopped
½ carrot, grated
1 small green chilli, chopped
2 tsp Dijon mustard
½ apple, diced

6 large lettuce leaves, washed well (for wrapping the egg salad)
A handful of purple/green grapes, halved
A fistful of nuts, chopped (optional)
Salt and pepper to taste

Method

Semi-boil eggs till they're two-thirds done (not completely cooked).
Yolks should be a bit soft.

Chop eggs finely. Add all the other ingredients to the eggs. Mix well to
ensure that the mixture is well coated with Dijon mustard.

Refrigerate it for 2–3 hours.

Put a dollop of egg salad on each lettuce leaf, roll it up and serve.

(Courtesy: Noopur Vijaya, Healthy Cooking Contest,
Food Stalking Group on Facebook)

Apple Blast

Ingredients

30 gms green apple, chopped
30 ml yogurt
1 tbsp honey

Method

Blend all the three ingredients together. Green apple smoothie is ready
to serve.

(Courtesy: Harmeen Bhatia of Dr Harmeen Bhatia's Homoeo-Health Clinic)

Fruit Power Smoothie (For Athletic Teenagers)

Ingredients

1 banana
½ apple
1 kiwi
1 cup orange juice
½ cup soy milk
½ cup plain yogurt
½ cup tofu

4 tsp peanut butter
2 tbsp aloe vera juice
2 tbsp flaxseeds

Method

Blend banana, apple, kiwi and orange juice until smooth.

Add soy milk, yogurt, tofu, peanut butter, aloe vera juice and flaxseeds until smooth.

(Courtesy: Harmeen Bhatia of Dr Harmeen Bhatia's Homoeo-Health Clinic)

Meal-Time Deals

Wholewheat Choco-chip Pancakes

Ingredients

1 ½ cups wholewheat flour
A little baking powder
¾ tsp salt
If making with eggs: 1¼ cups milk and 2 large eggs, lightly beaten
If making eggless: 1¾ cup yogurt, whisked
Little oil (preferably canola/olive) to grease non-stick pan
½ cup chocolate chips or freshly chopped chocolate of your choice

Method

In a large mixing bowl, combine all the ingredients, except the chocolate chips. The batter should be of pouring consistency but not watery or even too thick.

Heat a pan greased with a little oil on medium heat. Once heated, pour a ladle of batter on to the skillet. Sprinkle each pancake with chocolate chips.

Allow the pancake to cook on medium heat. You will notice the bubbles rising on the top side of pancake. At this point, flip the pancake and allow it to cook on the other side for about 30 seconds.

Flip again and serve hot.

(Courtesy: Anuradha Gaikwad, Healthy Cooking Contest,
Food Stalking Group on Facebook)

Healthy Oats Utthapam

Ingredients

2 cups oats
1 cup unsour curd
¼ cup sooji
2–3 green chillies, chopped
ginger–garlic paste to taste
A few curry leaves
Water, as needed
Salt to taste
1 tsp Eno (optional)

For the topping

Onion, tomato, capsicum, carrot, chopped finely

Method

Powder the oats in the blender.

Add curd to the oats powder.

Grind to a smooth paste and add water. Remove from blender.

Add sooji, chillies, ginger–garlic paste, curry leaves and salt and mix well.

Add Eno. If not, then keep it out for 45 minutes for fermentation.

The batter is ready. Spread it evenly on a hot skillet and cook till done.

Serve hot with coconut chutney/mint chutney.

(Courtesy: Anamika Khippal, Healthy Cooking Contest,
Food Stalking Group on Facebook)

Mexican Burrito Bowl

Ingredients

1 cup red kidney beans, boiled
1 cup mixed peppers, green, red, orange
½ cup onions, thinly sliced
1½ tbsp lemon juice
1 cup brown rice, cooked

½ cup fresh guacamole or mashed avocado
2 tbsp Greek yogurt (whisked)
2 sprigs coriander leaves
2 tbsp jalapeños, finely chopped
¼ cup sweet corn
½ cup spinach, shredded
cayenne pepper to taste
¼ cup salsa
Salt and pepper to taste

Method

Marinate red kidney beans, peppers and onion with lemon juice, salt, pepper and cayenne pepper for 4 hours or overnight (if possible).

Layer the serving dish with brown rice.

Place the marinated red kidney beans and shredded spinach.

Top with Greek yogurt, sweet corn, cilantro, jalapenos (according to taste) and salsa.

(Courtesy: Adya Shukla, Healthy Cooking Contest,
Food Stalking Group on Facebook)

Stuffed Mushrooms

Ingredients

10 button mushrooms
¼ cup capsicum (green, yellow and red), finely chopped
5 mushroom stems, finely chopped
¼ cup onion, finely chopped
A little parsley, finely chopped
Brown bread crumbs for binding
¼ cup Parmesan cheese
1–2 cloves garlic, grated
1-inch ginger, grated

Method

Remove stems from mushrooms and bake them for 10 minutes.

Prepare the filling by mixing capsicum, mushrooms stems, onions, parsley, bread crumbs, ginger and garlic.

Add half of the Parmesan cheese to the dry mixture.
Remove the mushrooms from the oven and fill the stuff.
Sprinkle the remaining Parmesan cheese on top of the mushrooms.
Bake for another 15 minutes.

(Courtesy: Adya Shukla, Healthy Cooking Contest,
Food Stalking Group on Facebook)

Palak Kadhi

Ingredients for Kadhi

1¼ cup sour curd
3 tbsp gram flour
1 tsp canola oil
4 red whole chillies
1 small onion, chopped
1 pinch of asafoetida
A little spinach, chopped
¼ tsp fenugreek seed
1 tsp ginger paste
1 tsp garlic paste
1½ tsp chilli powder
½ tsp turmeric powder
²/₃ cup water
Salt to taste

Ingredients for Pakodas

²/₃ cup gram flour
1 tsp chilli powder
1 onion, finely chopped
½ a bunch spinach, chopped
2 tbsp coriander leaves, finely chopped
Salt to taste
Air fryer or a pan

Method for Making Pakodas

In a mixing bowl, add gram flour along with chilli powder, salt, onions, chopped spinach and coriander leaves.

Add water little by little so that it can form a thick batter.

Make small balls from this batter and put them into an air fryer/appe pan.

Method for Making Kadhi

Take a big mixing bowl, whisk sour curd with gram flour and water. Make a smooth mixture without any lumps.

Add red chilli powder, turmeric and salt.

Heat oil in a kadai, add fenugreek seeds and asafoetida. Add whole red chillies, green chillies, ginger and garlic paste.

Add chopped onions and sauté them till they turn pink. Add spinach to the seasoning.

Stir well and add the sour curd mixer with one hand while stirring constantly with the other hand. Keep stirring to avoid lumping. Lower the heat, while stirring constantly till it starts boiling. Let it simmer for 10–15 minutes on low heat or till the kadhi becomes thick.

Now add the 'air-fried' pakodas to the kadhi and let them soak in the kadhi for some time.

Garnish it with the coriander leaves and serve hot with rice.

(Courtesy: Seema Rajput, Healthy Cooking Contest,
Food Stalking Group on Facebook)

Broccoli Salad

Ingredients

250 gm broccoli
100 gm cherry tomatoes
100 gm lettuce
100 gm almonds
30 gm feta cheese
2 tsp balsamic dressing
½ cup vinegar
½ cup balsamic vinegar
2 tsp mustard
3 cups olive oil

2 tsp black pepper
Salt to taste

Method for Balsamic Dressing

Mix vinegar, balsamic vinegar, mustard, olive oil, salt and pepper together and mix well.

Method for Broccoli Salad

Boil broccoli and cut tomatoes into small pieces.

Roast the almonds, chop the lettuce leaves.

Mix all the ingredients, then add balsamic dressing and feta cheese.

Garnish with roasted almonds.

(Courtesy: Harmeen Bhatia of Dr Harmeen Bhatia's Homoeo-Health Clinic)

Soy Bhurji

Ingredients

100 gm soya nuggets
Water to soak nuggets
1 tsp vinegar
¼ tsp black pepper powder
1 tsp olive oil
1 cup spring onions, chopped
1 cup tomatoes, chopped
1 tsp cumin seeds
1 tsp amchur
1 tsp chaat masala
Salt to taste

Method

Soak nuggets in water with vinegar added to it for ½ hour and drain. Mix together the nuggets, salt and black pepper and keep aside.

Heat a tsp of olive oil in a non-stick pan, add cumin seeds. When the seeds start to crackle, add onions, then add tomatoes after the onions are brown.

Now add nuggets and shallow fry for 3–4 minutes. Add amchur and chaat masala. Remove from heat.

Garnish with chopped coriander and serve hot.

(Courtesy: Harmeen Bhatia of Dr Harmeen Bhatia's Homoeo-Health Clinic, , Healthy Cooking Contest, Food Stalking Group on Facebook)

Dal-Palak Paneer Wholewheat Kathi Rolls

Ingredients for the Rolls

½ cup spinach puree (boiled and ground)
½ cup wholewheat flour
¹/₃ cup green chutney made with mint and coriander
3 tbsp date–tamarind chutney

Ingredients for Dal Layer

1 cup yellow moong dal
2 green chillies, finely chopped
¹/₃-inch ginger, finely chopped
salt to taste
water as needed

Ingredients for Vegetable Layer

1 small onion, finely chopped
1 cup mix of carrot, capsicum and beans, finely chopped
1 cup paneer, diced
A pinch of red chilli powder
¹/₃ tsp cumin seeds
¼ tsp turmeric powder
1 tbsp freshly squeezed lemon juice
1 tsp canola oil
Salt and pepper to taste

Method for Moong Dal

Soak moong dal overnight.

Grind it with chillies, ginger and salt.

Add water to make the batter of thick flowing consistency. Set aside.

Method for Roti

Knead wholewheat flour with spinach puree.

Make 3 rotis with the dough.

Method for Vegetables

Heat a non-stick pan and add canola oil. Add cumin seeds and let them crackle. Add onion and sauté till transparent and soft.

Add mixed vegetables and paneer. Sauté for 7–8 minutes on medium to slow flame till vegetables turn soft.

Add turmeric, red chillies, salt and pepper. Squeeze lemon juice and mix well.

Mash vegetables a little. Set aside.

Method for Kathi Rolls

Coat another pan lightly with canola oil and heat it.

Pour a ladle of moong batter.

Place a roti immediately on top of the batter and press to spread the batter on roti evenly on the edges.

Turn to see if the dal batter is cooked and dried.

Apply a layer of green chutney on the dal side of the roti.

Apply a tbsp of date–tamarind chutney over the green one.

Place one-third vegetable mixture over it.

Roll the roti and cut it into 2 halves and serve.

(Courtesy: Rashi Ahluwalia, Healthy Cooking Contest,
Food Stalking Group on Facebook)

Charwaha Chicken Pie

Ingredients

½ kg chicken mince
2 onions, chopped finely
2 tomatoes, pureed
2 potatoes, boiled
½ carrot, finely grated

2–3 leaves spinach, very finely chopped
1 tbsp ginger–garlic paste
2 tsp coriander powder
1 tsp chili powder
½ tsp turmeric powder
½ tsp garam masala
2 tbsp milk to moisten potatoes
1 tbsp oil
Salt to taste

Method

Heat oil in a non-stick kadai.

Add onions and sauté till brown.

Add ginger–garlic paste and sauté.

Add coriander powder, chilli, turmeric, garam masala and salt to taste.
Stir and cook for a few minutes.

Add the chicken mince. Fry till brown.

Now add tomato puree and cook again for a few minutes.

Mash potatoes in a separate bowl and add milk, carrot, spinach and a
little salt.

To Assemble

Preheat oven with top grill on at 250 degrees.

In an oven-proof dish, add one layer of mashed potatoes, add keema
over it. Now add the rest of the mash.

Grill in the oven for about 20 minutes or till it turns golden brown on
top. Charwaha pie is ready.

(Courtesy: Sharmila Nambiar, Healthy Cooking Contest,
Food Stalking Group on Facebook)

Pan-seared Salmon with Balsamic Reduction

Ingredients for Pan-seared Salmon

3 salmon fillets
1 tsp vinegar

2 tsp olive oil (or less)
2 tsp lemon juice
Salt and pepper to taste

Ingredients for Balsamic Reduction

3/4 cup balsamic vinegar
1 tbsp honey/maple syrup
1 tsp Dijon mustard

Method for Balsamic Reduction

Heat balsamic vinegar and let it simmer slowly.

Add honey/maple syrup and Dijon mustard.

Cook on low flame till the mix thickens to a beautiful glaze and starts to coat the back of a spoon.

Transfer to a bowl immediately as overcooking might burn the glaze beyond repair!

Method for Pan-seared salmon

Wash salmon fillets with vinegar. Pat dry with a paper towel.

Sprinkle with salt and pepper. Drizzle olive oil and lemon juice and leave for a few minutes. Meanwhile, heat oil in a flat-bottomed pan till really hot.

Place fillets alongside each other, taking care to leave some space between each fillet. Overcrowding will prevent the fish from acquiring a good sear.

Reduce heat to medium and cook for 4 minutes. Flip and cook for another 3–4 minutes on the other side. Transfer to serving platter.

Drizzle liberally with balsamic reduction. Serve warm.

(Courtesy: Ruchi Airen, Blog: Foodfellas 4 YOU)

The Verdict

I have endeavoured to share recipes for healthy snacks and main meals to appeal to a diverse assortment of young palates. This potpourri is an outcome of the labour of various mums with fussy children of their own, who finally hit the jackpot with these recipes. So, if you sail in a similar boat, experiment, innovate, or simply Google for zestful and savoury dishes with a motley of flavours—you are sure to get lucky. As they say, variety is the spice of life. It may be a cliché, but a wide selection of food definitely makes eating an interesting activity for kids and eases the woes of parents of fussy eaters.

Chapter 16
Myth-Busters
Demystifying Ten Common Nutritional Fallacies

The field of nutrition is perpetually barraged with incessant information on what to eat and what not to eat, when to eat, how to eat and so on. Often, the information is self-contradictory, leaving the reader utterly baffled. In such a scenario of over-information, it is not at all surprising to expect muddled minds seeking 'the actual truth', especially when it concerns their little ones' health and diet. So, I intend to burst the bubble around ten common misconceptions that surround child nutrition.

Myth 1: Carbohydrates are edible enemies that bloat the little bellies up!

Reality: All carbohydrates are not evil guys. In fact, of the three macronutrients in our diet—namely, carbohydrates, protein and fats—carbohydrates are the body's primary source of energy. It's especially essential for kids to have a carb-rich diet to maintain high energy levels while studying, playing and exercising. Carbohydrates greatly impact the concentration levels of children and a low-carb diet would mean lower concentration. Roughly 70 per cent of the daily calories for kids should come from complex carbohydrates like fruits, vegetables, brown rice, whole grains, multigrain or wholewheat bread, whole grain roti, sweet potato, dried and fresh beans and legumes. The ones to be given a cold-shoulder are simple carbohydrates such as table sugar, white bread, refined flour, white pasta, white rice, sugary cereals, fruit juices and candy, which are nutritionally empty and need to be avoided.

Myth 2: Fat is the Usual Suspect. Keep him off, kids!

Reality: Fat, again, has two faces—the saintly and the beastly.
You should be able to tell good fat from the bad fat, as eliminating
fat completely from a child's diet is not an option. Saturated
fats and trans fats are the villains that push us towards heart
ailments; while MUFA (mono-unsaturated fatty acids) and
PUFA (poly-unsaturated fatty acids) are the guardian angels
that care for our health. Saturated fats are present in foods like
red meat, processed meat products, dairy products like cream,
creamy cheese and butter; coconut, coconut oil and palm oil.
Trans fats are foods like burgers, fried chicken, French fries, all
fried food, cookies, cakes and chips. The most effective
replacements for these bad fats are PUFA (safflower, soybean,
sunflower and sesame oils, fish, flaxseeds and walnuts) and
MUFA (sesame seeds, soybean and sunflower seed oils, almonds,
peanuts, pecans, hazelnuts and macadamia nuts, pistachios,
cashews and Brazil nuts). These lower coronary heart disease
risk and increase good cholesterol.

Myth 3: Snack all day! Any time is snack time!

Reality: While some snacking is beneficial, kids today typically
snack all day long. Snacking wouldn't be worrisome if kids were
munching on healthful, nutrient-rich foods. Ideal snacks would
be multigrain vegetable or cheese sandwiches, vegetable upma,
red rice poha, fruit, vegetable fingers with a healthy dip, vegetable
juice, peanut butter sandwich and trail-mix. But alas! This was
not to be. Childhood snacking trends are moving towards
almost three snacks per day as compared to the one healthy
snack per day, which children usually had about thirty years
ago. Now fried packaged food, cookies, cakes, candy, desserts
and sweetened beverages proliferate and are the major source of
calories. These could contribute in great measure to fat gain.
Overweight children and teenagers are also at a higher risk of

developing serious diseases such as type 2 diabetes and heart disease.

Myth 4: Juices are the fountainhead of good health...let them flow through the day!

Reality: However vitamin-rich and healthy the fruit from which juice is extracted may be, fruit juice still takes a beating from the whole fruit, which is fibrous and filling. Fruit juices are nothing but concentrated sources of sugar which don't give the children the same level of nutrients that they would get from whole fruits. Instead, kids end up consuming a whole lot of calories through juices, while their hunger still persists. Fruit juices also lack fibre that keeps the appetite satiated for a longer period. They spike up energy levels quickly, but are quicker in bringing about a dip in blood sugar, which leads to a fall in energy levels. So, give a juicy fruit to your little ones instead of juices for optimum health benefits. But if fruit juices must be had, this is what you should do:

❑ Tone down the sugar calories by watering the juice down to around a 50:50 ratio.

❑ Offer only fresh fruit juices without added sugar instead of commercially packed juices. Commercial juices are a concentrated source of sugar, loaded with preservatives and hardly have any real fruit in them, containing mostly fruit flavours in the garb of real fruit.

❑ Offer juices only occasionally. Don't get your child into a habit that is difficult to break later on.

Myth 5: A multivitamin a day is a magic bullet for all afflictions!

Reality: People tend to think that a daily multivitamin is a good health insurance for children. They forget that it's only a *supplement* that is meant to complement the diet and not a proxy for the foods that one doesn't eat. What's more, taking too many supplements and evading natural foods can end up sabotaging your child's future health. It also means that your child is going to miss out on the synergistic health effects that can only come from a variety of whole and natural foods. The 'pill-nutrition' also gives a wrong signal to kids that food can be ditched, as the 'magic pill' will make up for the lack of food and keep them healthy. So, don't supplement your child's diet with individual supplements without the guidance of your doctor as multivitamins are definitely not a cure-all for a poor diet.

Myth 6: 'Clean your plate' is the non-negotiable virtue! Teach them early!

Reality: Young children usually stop eating when they feel full and parents shouldn't override these natural eating cues. Serving adult-size portions and encouraging children to eat more than they want can lead to negative eating behaviour patterns in later years. This treatment may condition them in their growing years to finish whatever is served in their plate, even if they're feeling full to their throats. This is also a major source of obesity. So, try serving your child half of an adult-sized portion and allow your child to stop eating when she feels satisfied.

Myth 7: Kids are special! Their meals should be too!

Reality: It's a fallacy that kids' and adults' tastes are as dissimilar as night and day. And it is even a bigger fallacy that kids need special kid-friendly foods. Children have no predetermined tastes and can learn to eat almost everything that parents eat. This is the stage for them to develop preferences for certain foods. So, if your child is offered mostly sweet, salty, bland, or fatty foods, then he or she will grow up with a taste for such foods. The food industry is also to blame for misleading parents by convincing them through brilliant marketing that kids will only eat kiddies' foods which are highly processed, sugary, or salty fast foods. So, don't be hoodwinked by the ubiquitous advertisements that lure your children into making wrong food choices. Instead, start them off in life with positive eating habits by introducing them to different foods, tastes and textures early. From then on, you can gradually increase the variety of nutrients in your child's diet.

Myth 8: Full-fat milk is the only champion, all the rest are unworthy losers!

Reality: It's full-fat milk only for two-year-olds and below. The sole purpose is to fill them up on fat that is needed until the age of two for nerve and brain development. After the age of two, if children have a varied and balanced diet and seem to be growing normally, they can move to consuming low-fat/toned/skimmed milk. Only an underweight child, who is a poor eater, should continue drinking full-fat milk. Full-fat milk is saturated fat that can lead to clogging of arteries, resulting in heart disease in adulthood.

Myth 9: Adults and pre-schoolers alike: 'Dieting' is the only mantra to shed kilos!

Reality: It's sad that some over-enthusiastic parents put their overweight pre-schoolers on a low-fat or low-carb diet because putting a small child on such a rigid diet is counter-productive and can have far-reaching negative effects. Here's a rundown on the two types of diets, that is, a low-fat diet and a low-carb one.

Low-fat diets can prove to be life-threatening for children, as good fats are essential for growth, tissue repair and cellular health. Instead, what is required is the careful elimination of bad fats from the child's diet, omitting food items such as full-fat dairy products, desserts, heavy milkshakes, high-calorie salad dressings, fried foods and red meat.

Low-carb diets can be equally dangerous as carbohydrates are essentially the most important source of energy for kids. Here too, it is the bad carbs that need to be eliminated from your child's diet, such as white bread, refined flour and its products, fizzy drinks, cakes, cookies, burgers and pizzas.

The mistake parents often make is that they feed their pre-schoolers as if they were teenagers. You only need to make some lifestyle changes to their daily routine. Some of these are: exercise portion control, offer five to six smaller meals through the day, offer more fruits and salads, cut down on junk and calorie-dense foods and add exercise to their routine.

Myth 10: Need iron? Red meat it is. Look no further!

Reality: There is no denying that iron is a critical nutrient for your child's growth and development and that red meat is an excellent source of iron, but your child can get adequate iron from many other foods too, like seafood, poultry, fish, beans, whole grain or enriched cereal, lentils, legumes, dried fruits, seeds, nuts, tofu and green leafy vegetables. Red meat is the main dietary source of high blood cholesterol and if consumed frequently, it could raise bad cholesterol levels (LDL) when the child grows up, which in turn could lead to serious heart ailments.

The Verdict

There is no denying the fact that we often believe what over-zealous marketing endorses, especially since most parents are not nutritional experts. Though it's easier to follow this herd instinct, we should dissect the information given and verify each of these beliefs from more authentic sources, as it is our precious children whose health is at stake.

There are enough nutritional fallacies promoted as good health caveats floating all around us which are quite possibly false and come in the way of a balanced diet for kids. Parents need to be discerning enough not to take all tall nutritional claims at face value. The solution: check out authentic websites and reach out to your child's paediatrician or nutritionist to get an unambiguous view.

Chapter 17

Exercise

The Elixir of Life

Hide-and-seek, hop-scotch, leap frog...anyone? Silence. No takers! TV, Xbox, smartphones, iPads...anyone? OH YES! All hands raised! This is the deplorable state many children are in today. While our generation's most precious childhood memories are riveted on simple outdoor fun activities like chasing each other with aimless giggles, climbing up a tree, skipping rope, cycling and playing made-up games, children today are fixated on and fettered to screens almost infinitely. They are at an immense risk of passing their childhood by, not ever learning about simple joys untainted by technology! How can we blame these children when many of us as parents are oblivious to the perils of 'gadgetdiction'!

So, what are the dangers of letting our kids get tangled in the gizmo world?

Pitfalls of Technological Overindulgence

Gadget addiction: I have seen it all around me. Children are so fixated to these hand-held gizmos that they find it almost agonizing to put them down even after extended hours of play. All entreaties by hassled parents fall on deaf ears. Their obsession causes behavioural problems, making them snappy and aggressive when asked to drop the device.

Attention deficit disorder: Due to gizmo addiction, many kids are distracted from paying attention to academics. This has become the prime cause for the fast-spreading Attention Deficit Disorder (ADD). Children suffering from ADD find it difficult to focus on academics or any other such activity needing concentration. This is likely to adversely affect their knowledge-enhancement and school grades.

Creativity: Children have become reluctant to read books and engage in creative games or other such activities. Their imagination, creativity, mental agility and, even, sense of humour don't seem to come into play. They are reluctant to tax their brains because they have no patience for anything but playing with these gadgets, which give them an instant fix.

Health jeopardy: Relentless use of gadgetry can bring on a slew of health problems for youngsters. Some of these are:

- ❏ *Obesity:* Their sedentary lifestyle makes these kids couch potatoes, dissuading them from any form of physical activity. This is bound to make them overweight.
- ❏ *Declining eyesight:* Undue strain to the eyes by staring at gadget screens for extended hours can cause eye problems.
- ❏ *Hearing troubles:* Constant blaring music from earphones attached to gadgets can make kids hard of hearing, which is a matter of concern.
- ❏ *Sharp headaches:* Incessantly staring at the gadget screen can cause severe headaches.
- ❏ *Sleep disorders:* When children continue to use these modern gizmos right up to bedtime, their sleep patterns get totally disturbed, leading to erratic sleep and sometimes to insomnia at a young age.
- ❏ *Flawed posture:* Children who sit for extended hours in one position while playing with gadgets can develop a poor sitting posture, causing severe pain to the spine, neck and shoulders.

Social reclusiveness: Children who are deeply trapped inside their gadget world are at a serious risk of becoming unsociable and cynical. It is very difficult for these kids to enjoy normal friendships and social interactions because they socialize in the virtual world through social networking sites. This habit is bound to worsen with passing years if there is no intervention to break it. They may become loners, with very few friends in the real world and may have problems settling down in society when they grow up.

Low self-esteem: Isolation can submerge self-esteem considerably, affecting a child's self-confidence adversely. Low self-esteem can even batter the emotional development of the child, making him feel emotionally inadequate.

How amazing is the fact that a park or a mere stretch of road in your vicinity can rejuvenate your child by helping him breathe fresh air, make some friends and gain health? And this is definitely not all. Here are some of the benefits of stepping outside the tightly clamped doors of the technical world into the vast openness of nature.

Benefits of Stepping Out

Physical development: Kids who step out of their homes to play for at least an hour every day are healthier, fitter and more energetic than those who don't. Their metabolism is much higher and they end up burning more calories and strengthening their muscles. Outdoor play also increases their flexibility, sense of balance and gross motor skills. It also builds up their bone mass.

Social development: Outdoor play also promotes social interaction and teamwork. Kids have more opportunities to interact with each other without even realizing that they are socializing. They grow up to be amiable and helpful individuals rather than stand-offish and self-centred beings. They also learn to share and become more patient when interacting with others.

Stress reduction: Regular exposure to sunlight calms one down and reduces stress. It is a major mood-enhancer, which is why a 'good nature' of a person is referred to as a 'sunny disposition'. Teacher and child advocate Leslie Gilbert-Lurie in her article '10 Ways to Minimize your Child's Stress' advises parents to encourage outdoor physical activity, which helps to reduce stress and strike a balance between the body and mind. Outdoor play also reduces boredom and cuts the risk of depression.

Increase in confidence: Physical activity also helps develop a sense of confidence and builds self-esteem in children as they make new friends and also become fitter for all to see.

Improvement of perceptual skills: These are abilities such as smell, hearing and touch. By observing the pattern on a leaf, smelling a fragrant flower, listening to singing birds, feeling the texture of sand, plucking a fruit from a tree and tasting it, children will not only sharpen their visual, auditory, tactile, olfactory and taste senses, but will also perk up their imagination and creativity. Outdoor play enhances their sense of wonder in the world around them.

Improves concentration and academic performance: Many children shun outdoor play and fitness activities before and during exams to 'concentrate' on studies. Does exercise really jar with academics? It, in fact, is a great way to de-stress from academic pressure and take a mental break from studies, especially around exam time. It can refresh children and enhance their focus. So, I strongly believe that playing outdoors complements learning in a very positive way.

ADHD control: Outdoor play is known to help the kids develop self-control and improve health conditions such as the Attention Deficit Hyperactivity Disorder (ADHD). Psychotherapist Terry Matlen says, 'Children who are hyperactive and impulsive can release tension far easier while outside running, jumping, swinging and playing sports than while sitting indoors.' 'Exercise increases dopamine levels in the brain and these levels are naturally low in the ADHD brain,' says Stephanie Sarkis, PhD, a psychotherapist and author of several books on ADHD, such as *Making the Grade with ADD: A Student's Guide to Succeeding in College with Attention Deficit Disorder.*

Fifteen Fun Ideas for Your Child to Explore the Exciting Outdoors

After throwing some light upon the various disadvantages of gadget fixation and merits of playing outdoors, I now need to talk about a few stimulating outdoor ideas that can be happily explored by children so as to deluge them with positivity and good health. Besides the innumerable regular fitness activities that are available in the neighbourhood such as tennis, swimming, basketball, cricket, taekwondo, skating, squash, sprints, aerobics, Zumba, yoga, soccer and volleyball, let us explore some of the other fun ideas for our children:

1. Encourage your child to surrender half the time from her screen-time daily. Prevail upon her to play unstructured games outdoors, such as hop-scotch, hide-and-seek, four corners, jump rope, Simon says and any other simple game. Jog your childhood memory to come up with more such games for them.

2. Go for a walk at least once a week on a muddy, shrubby trail with your child. Allow him to explore. Do not hamper his trail of thoughts or offer assistance unless asked for.

3. Send your little one to the nearby garden or park with a notebook and a bag to collect 'wild treasures' like cones, peculiarly shaped leaves, pebbles and so on. Encourage her to make note of anything interesting that she observes. She could even click pictures if she wants to.

4. Encourage your young ones to feed birds. This will get them closer to loving and caring for other living beings. Besides, feeding birds is a great stress-buster.

5. Help your child to organize a 'trash pick-up hour' within your neighbourhood along with his buddies. They could go out with a garbage bag each to pick up things like dry leaves, stones, food wrappers, plastic objects, or sharp and dangerous objects from the residential paths.

6. Take your child out on a bright and sunny winter morning during vacations every day for an hour, to sunbathe while observing the natural environment and to play games like Frisbee or hand ball in the park. This will also ensure that they absorb the vitamin from sunshine—vitamin D.

7. Encourage your child to go bug-watching with a magnifying glass. Ask her to take pictures or draw them. Later, she could identify the species by searching through the net.

8. Go on a biking spree or a run with your child. Exchange jokes and funny anecdotes, and laugh together on the way to make it a fun. Young adults can even fix a day in a week to bike all the way to school and back if the school rules, distance and other circumstances permit.

9. Visit a zoo with your little one. Children are fascinated by a variety of animals. This is a fun way for your child to learn about animal behaviour, their food, sounds and habits.

10. Send your older child to run an errand for you, like buying vegetables, fruits and milk from a neighbouring departmental store once a week. This will not only make her feel more responsible and give a sense of importance, but will also make her aware of seasonal foods and their prices.

11. If you have a pet dog, persuade your child to walk the dog outside at least once every day. Encourage her to playfully run with it or play ball with it. This will also ensure that both your child and your pet end up getting some exercise.

12. Let your child and his friends learn how to fly a kite during the kite-flying season. Flying a kite will not only give your child a real high, but will also help him exercise his upper body.

13. Even if you're at home, just turn on your favourite dance music and swing and sway to the beats with your little child. It is a fun way to shed extra calories and unwind at the same time.

14. Encourage your child to plant a sapling in your residential area with the help of a local gardener. He and his friends can even volunteer to water the plants around their residential blocks every Sunday. This could hone his gardening skills in the bargain.

15. Plan to go star-gazing one night along with your child. Coordinate with some amateur/professional astronomers in the area who could lend or rent out their telescopes and binoculars.

The Verdict

Outdoor activities provide children with a perfect platform for discovering and experimenting with the wide world outside their homes to expand their horizons.

Remember, children are naturally drawn to active play outdoors. But we as parents need to show them the way to this spectacular world, pulling them away from a sedentary lifestyle that can lead to umpteen illnesses. We can facilitate this by stringently scheduling fitness activities into the calendar and committing some family time each week to enjoy the brighter and more positive world outside the four walls of our homes.

Even holidays can be made more fun and meaningful for the whole family by planning short hikes or treks. Run with your children on the beach sand if it's a seaside holiday or trek on mountain trails. When there are no holidays, brisk walks with the family in the evening or after dinner could be the option.

Once children learn to love outdoor physical activities because of regular exposure to them, they are likely to carry these healthy interests into their adulthood. So, help them break free from the shackles of the screens that lure them away from the simple pleasures of being carefree kids—and give them wings!

Glossary of Terms

Allspice: Garam masala
Amaranth: Rajgira/ramdana
Anchovy: Capsali mandli
Apricot: Khoobani
Avocado: Makhanphal
Barley: Jau
Bell peppers: Capsicum
Black-eyed beans: Lobia
Bran: Choker
Broken wheat porridge: Daliya
Buckwheat: Kuttu
Bulgur wheat porridge: Daliya
Cantaloupe: Kharbuja
Catfish: Singhara
Cayenne pepper: Red chillies
Chia seeds: Sabja
Chickpeas: Kabuli chana
Coconut flesh: Nariyal malai
Cod fish: Gobro
Colocasia: Arbi
Cottage cheese: Paneer
Cracked wheat: Daliya
Dried peas: Matra
Edamame: Green or kachchi soybean
Finger millet: Ragi/nachni
Fresh green garbanzos: Chholiya
Fresh milk cream: Malai
Garbanzo beans: Kabuli chana
Grapefruit: Chakotra
Guacamole: Mexican dip made of avocado
Halibut: Bakas
Herring: Bhing

Honeydew melon: Kharbuja
Indian gooseberry: Amla
Kelp: Sivar
Kidney beans: Rajma
Lentils: Dals
Lima beans: Sem phalli
Mackerel: Bangda
Muskmelon: Kharbuja
Navy beans: White rajma
Parsley: Ajmoda
Pearl millet: Bajra
Pinto beans: Spotted rajma
Plantain: Unripe banana
Refined flour: Maida
Ridge gourd: Torai
Sago: Saboodana
Salmon: Rawas
Sardine: Pedvey
Seaweeds: Samudri shaiwal
Semolina: Sooji
Sesame seeds: Til
Shrimp: Jheenga
Sorghum: Jowar
Sprouted lentils: Ankurit dal
Sweetmeats: Mithai
Sweet potato: Shakarkandi
Tuna: Chura
Turnip greens: Shaljam saag
Wheat germ: Gehu ka ankur
White beans: Safed sem
Wood apple: Bel
Zucchini: Torai

Bibliography

Chapter 1: A Goulash of Good Health

The Eat Well Plate

http://www.nhs.uk/Livewell/Goodfood/Pages/eatwell-plate.aspx

http://www.healthystart.nhs.uk/food-and-health-tips/healthy-eating-eatwell-plate/

http://www.cdc.gov/healthyweight/assessing/bmi/childrens_bmi/about_childrens_bmi.html

A Balanced Diet

http://www.choosemyplate.gov/

http://www.betterhealth.vic.gov.au/bhcv2/bhcarticles.nsf/pages/Eating_tips_for_children_(5)_primary_school?open

http://fnic.nal.usda.gov/dietary-guidance/dietary-reference-intakes/dri-tables

http://www.mayoclinic.org/healthy-lifestyle/childrens-health/in-depth/nutrition-for-kids/art-20049335

http://www.bbcgoodfood.com/howto/guide/healthy-eating-what-young-children-need

http://kidshealth.org/parent/nutrition_center/healthy_eating/habits.html

http://www.nhs.uk/Livewell/Goodfood/Pages/Healthyeating.aspx

http://www.webmd.com/children/guide/kids-healthy-eating-habits

Chapter 2: The Incredibles 1

https://www.nrv.gov.au/chronic-disease/macronutrient-balance http://healthy-kids.com.au/kids/high-school-2/macronutrients/

https://www.nrv.gov.au/nutrients/fats-total-fat-fatty-acids

http://kidshealth.org/parent/growth/feeding/sugar.html

http://kidshealth.org/parent/growth/feeding/fat.html

http://healthyeating.sfgate.com/sources-fats-toddlers-3964.html

https://www.healthychildren.org/English/healthy-living/nutrition/Pages/What-About-Fat-And-Cholesterol.aspx

http://kidshealth.org/kid/nutrition/food/protein.html

http://healthyeating.sfgate.com/highprotein-foods-kids-eat-9997.html

Chapter 3: The Incredibles 2

http://projecthealthychildren.org/why-food-fortification/micronutrients/

http://www.cdc.gov/immpact/micronutrients/

http://www.ncbi.nlm.nih.gov/pubmed/11509111

http://www.webmd.com/parenting/child-nutrition-13/slideshow-essential-nutrients

http://www.webmd.com/diet/healthy-kitchen-11/10-missing-nutrients

Chapter 4: Fibre in the Belly

http://kidshealth.org/parent/growth/feeding/fiber.html

http://www.aboutkidshealth.ca/en/healthaz/healthandwellness/nutrition/pages/higher-fibre-diet.aspx

http://healthyeating.sfgate.com/foods-highest-fiber-roughage-1132.html

http://www.livestrong.com/article/394469-list-of-roughage-foods/

Chapter 5: Nutrient-infused, Immunity-boosting Heroes

http://www.betterhealth.vic.gov.au/bhcv2/bhcarticles.nsf/pages/Childrens_diet_fruit_and_vegetables?open

http://healthyeating.sfgate.com/benefits-fruits-vegetables-kids-6463.html

http://www.livestrong.com/article/408292-what-are-the-benefits-of-fruits-vegetables-for-kids/

https://www.healthykids.nsw.gov.au/kids-teens/eat-more-fruit-and-vegies-kids.aspx

Chapter 6: That Divine Cooler

http://kidshealth.org/kid/stay_healthy/food/water.html

http://www.nutrition.org.uk/healthyliving/hydration/hydration-for-children.html

http://www.naturalhydrationcouncil.org.uk/hydration-facts/hydration-and-water-facts-for-kids-2/

https://www.healthykids.nsw.gov.au/kids-teens/stats-and-facts-teens/teens-nutrition/drinks-for-hydration.aspx

Chapter 7: The Dreaded Trinity

Sugar

http://www.mayoclinic.org/healthy-lifestyle/nutrition-and-healthy-eating/expert-blog/kids-and-sugar/bgp-20056149

http://www.nhs.uk/Livewell/Goodfood/Pages/sugars.aspx

http://healthyeating.sfgate.com/negative-effects-refined-sugar-children-7164.html

http://healthyeating.sfgate.com/maximum-amount-sugar-day-children-8982.html

http://www.who.int/nutrition/sugars_public_consultation/en/

Salt

http://www.dietitians.ca/Nutrition-Resources-A-Z/Factsheets/Minerals/Food-Sources-of-Sodium.aspx

http://www.news-medical.net/news/20120521/Salt-intake-why-is-it-bad-for-you.aspx

http://www.bloodpressureuk.org/microsites/salt/Home/Whysaltisbad

http://www.webmd.com/hypertension-high-blood-pressure/news/20150313/salt-may-be-bad-for-more-than-your-blood-pressure

http://www.worldactiononsalt.com/salthealth/children/

http://www.awash.org.au/for-consumers/salt-and-children/

http://www.nhs.uk/Livewell/Goodfood/Pages/salt.aspx

Fat

http://www.ncbi.nlm.nih.gov/pubmed/10645998

http://www.nhs.uk/Livewell/Goodfood/Pages/Fat.aspx

http://kidshealth.org/parent/growth/feeding/fat.html

http://www.nutrition.org.uk/healthyliving/basics/fats.html

http://raisingchildren.net.au/articles/fat_basics.html/context/218

Chapter 8: Food for Thought

http://www.webmd.com/add-adhd/childhood-adhd/features/brain-foods-kids

http://www.webmd.com/parenting/features/brain-foods-for-children

http://www.prevention.com/food/food-remedies/best-foods-kids-brains

http://www.medicinenet.com top_10_brain_foods_for_children_pictures_slideshow/article.htm

http://www.eatingwell.com/nutrition_health/healthy_aging/foods_that_boost_brain_power

Chapter 9: Fuel for the Fitness Fanatics

The Dietary Requirements of Young Athletes

http://www.ncbi.nlm.nih.gov/pmc/articles/PMC3805623/

http://kidshealth.org/parent/nutrition_center/dietary_needs/feed_child_athlete.html

http://www.webmd.com/fitness-exercise/nutrition-tips-athletes

http://www.mayoclinic.org/healthy-lifestyle/nutrition-and-healthy-eating/expert-blog/sports-nutrition-tips/bgp-20056130

Sports Hydration

http://www.webmd.com/parenting/active-child-hydrated

http://www.webmd.com/fitness-exercise/drink-up-sports-fitness

http://kidshealth.org/parent/nutrition_center/healthy_eating/power_drinks.html

http://www.mayoclinic.org/healthy-lifestyle/tween-and-teen-health/in-depth/dehydration/art-20047470

http://www.aboutkidshealth.ca/En/HealthAZ/HealthandWellness/Nutrition/Pages/Sports-Nutrition.aspx

http://www.mayoclinic.org/healthy-lifestyle/tween-and-teen-health/in-depth/dehydration/art-20047470

Chapter 10: Beyond Mamma's Kitchen

http://kidshealth.org/teen/food_fitness/nutrition/eating_out.html

http://healthycanadians.gc.ca/eating-nutrition/healthy-eating-saine-alimentation/tips-conseils/eating-out-manger-exterieur-eng.php

https://www.eatrightontario.ca/en/Articles/Child-Toddler-Nutrition/You-can-ask——for-healthy-foods-for-your-kids

http://www.webmd.com/cholesterol-management/guide/healthy-choices-when-eating-out

http://www.parenting.com/toddler/feeding-nutrition/dining-out-kids-healthy-eating-dont-have-to-be-mutually-exclusive

http://www.health.harvard.edu/blog/think-fast-when-kids-want-fast-food-201301315846

http://www.nhlbi.nih.gov/health/educational/wecan/eat-right/eating-out.htm

http://www.eatright.org/resource/health/weight-loss/eating-out/eating-out

Chapter 11: Fat Boy Slim, Mission Possible

http://www.who.int/mediacentre/factsheets/fs311/en/

http://www.ncbi.nlm.nih.gov/pmc/articles/PMC3028965/

http://www.who.int/end-childhood-obesity/facts/en/

http://obesityfoundationindia.com/index.htm

http://timesofindia.indiatimes.com/life-style/health-fitness/health-news/Obesity-in-kids-on-the-rise-in-Mumbai/movie-review/27576055.cms

http://www.cdc.gov/healthyweight/children/

http://www.fda.gov/ForConsumers/ConsumerUpdates/ucm229990.htm

https://www.health.ny.gov/prevention/nutrition/resources/obparnts.htm

http://www.webmd.com/children/preventing-childhood-obesity

http://www.ncbi.nlm.nih.gov/pmc/articles/PMC3063535/

Chapter 12: Help! My Child is All Skin and Bones

http://www.nhs.uk/Livewell/Goodfood/Pages/Underweightyoungchild.aspx

http://healthyeating.sfgate.com/nutrition-recommendations-underweight-kids-6671.html

http://www.eatright.org/resource/health/weight-loss/your-health-and-your-weight/safe-weight-gain-tips-for-underweight-kids

http://www.mayoclinic.org/healthy-lifestyle/nutrition-and-healthy-eating/expert-answers/underweight/faq-20058429

Chapter 13: Picky Palates

http://www.mayoclinic.org/healthy-lifestyle/childrens-health/in-depth/childrens-health/art-20044948

Chapter 14: Snack Attack

Credit lines have been offered within the text

Chapter 15: Bite Me, I'm Bliss!

Credit lines have been offered within the text

Chapter 16: Myth-Busters

https://well.wvu.edu/articles/10_dieting_myths

http://www.sidra.org/unveiling-childhood-nutrition-myths-for-national-nutrition-month/

http://www.abc.net.au/health/talkinghealth/factbuster/stories/2013/02/07/3685289.htm

http://www.health.com/health/article/0,,20430359,00.html

http://www.virginiahopkinstestkits.com/kids_nutrition_dr_john_lee.html

Chapter 17: Exercise

http://psychcentral.com/blog/archives/2013/06/01/outdoor-activities-for-kids-with-adhd/

http://outdoornation.org.uk/2013/05/22/are-children-losing-touch-with-nature-and-does-it-matter-if-they-are/

http://www.nationaltrust.org.uk/article-1356398566853/

http://www.dnaindia.com/health/report-are-mobile-phones-and-tablets-ruining-your-childs-development-1871227

http://www.telegraph.co.uk/technology/10008707/Toddlers-becoming-so-addicted-to-iPads-they-require-therapy.html

Acknowledgements

First and foremost, my book-writing journey couldn't have happened without divine intervention. God proposed that I put my spare time to good use, and the book emerged. I am ever grateful to my Lord for planting the seed.

While the immortal power above willed me to write, I couldn't have made significant headway without the timely nudge of a few mortals very close to my heart and soul. I am ever grateful and indebted to them for being a continual part of my book-writing voyage. Thank you Charanjit Singh Sodhi (my husband) and Angad Singh Sodhi (my son) for lending constant support, enduring my numerous mood swings and still being patient and indulgent from start to finish.

Appendix

A General Calorie Chart

Here is a grid that gives you an approximate calorie count of various foods that are consumed as part of our children's day-to-day diet. The foods are categorized on the basis of the various nutrients they contain (carbohydrates, proteins, fats, dairy, fruits and vegetables) for easy reference. This will be a handy guide for you while rating and evaluating the nutrient value of various foods so as to plan your child's daily diet systematically. This grid also gives the approximate calorie count of some common junk foods to help you to realize the extent of the damage caused by consuming them.

Fruits	Calories
1 Banana	107
1 Mango	135
1 Litchi	11
1 Apple	95
1 Orange	60
Grapes (1 cup)	110
1 Kiwi	46
1 Guava	46
1 Hard Pear	48
Strawberries (1 cup)	45
Gooseberries (100gm)	58
Watermelon (1 cup)	46
1 Lemon	17
Muskmelon (1 cup)	54
1 Peach	42
1 Pomegranate	105
Pineapple (1 cup)	76
Plum (1 medium)	30
1 Tomato	25
1 Soft Pear	98
1 Cheeku	170
Papaya (1 cup)	90

Fruits	Calories
Cherries (1 cup)	87
Jamun (100gms)	62
1 Sweet Lime	43
1 Fresh Date	70
Raw Coconut (1 cup)	283

Carbohydrates	Calories
Wheat Porridge in water (1 cup)	140
Whole Moong Dal, cooked (1 cup)	320
Toor Dal, cooked (1 cup)	203
White Rice, cooked (1 cup)	205
Brown Rice, cooked (1 cup)	216
Wheat Porridge in Milk (1 cup)	241
Wheat Porridge Upma (1 cup)	170
1 Roti	106
White Bread (1 slice)	66
Wholewheat Bread (1 slice)	69
Multigrain Bread (1 slice)	70
Oatmeal with Water (1 cup)	166
Oatmeal with Milk and Honey (1 cup)	270
Cornflakes with Skimmed Milk (1 cup)	170
Chocos with Skimmed Milk (1 cup)	215
Unsweetened Apple Juice (1 glass)	117
Unsweetened Grape Juice (1 cup)	154
Unsweetened Orange Juice (1 cup)	110
Unsweetened Pomegranate Juice (1 cup)	134
Unsweetened Pineapple Juice (1 cup)	140
Unsweetened Lemon Juice (1 cup)	60

Proteins	Calories
1 Egg whole (large)	74
1 Egg white (large)	17
Chicken, cooked (1 cup)	344
Mutton, cooked (1 cup)	391
Pork, cooked (1 cup)	363
Beef Steak, cooked (1 cup)	338
Lentil Sprouts (1 cup)	31

Proteins	Calories
Fish Type (100 gms each)	
Salmon	146
Sole	117
Pomfret	102
Tuna	128
Sardines	217
Snapper	110
Mackerel	167
Herring	242
Trout	188

Vegetables	Calories
Potato (1 medium)	161
Tomato (1 raw)	33
Spinach (1 cup)	41
Beetroot (1 cup)	75
Carrot (1 raw)	30
Radish (1 cup)	20
1 Cucumber	45
Green Beans, boiled (1 cup)	44
Capsicum (1 cup)	30
Broccoli (1 cup raw)	44
Cabbage (1 cup raw)	18
Cauliflower (1 cup)	30
Eggplant, boiled (1 cup)	22
Lotus Stem (1 cup)	78
Sweet Potato (1 cup)	180
Mushrooms (1 cup)	15
Onion (1 cup)	64
Peas (1 cup)	124

Fats	Calories
Milk Whole (1 cup)	146
Milk Skimmed (1 cup)	80
Cheddar Cheese (1 slice)	113
Cream Cheese (1 tbsp)	51
Heavy Cream (1 cup)	821

Fats	Calories
Skim Milk Cream (1 cup)	80
Ghee (1 tbsp)	112
Butter (1 tbsp)	102
Cooking Oil (1 tbsp)	115

Junk Food	Calories
McDonald's Chicken Burger	525
McDonald's McVeggies Burger	424
Chicken McNuggets (1 piece)	44
KFC Fried Chicken Breast	380
KFC Fried Chicken Drumstick	140
KFC Chicken Popcorn (large)	560
French Fries (large)	685
French Fries (medium)	487
French Fries (small)	343
Pizza Hut Chicken Pizza (1 slice)	610
Pizza Hut Plain Cheese Pizza (1 slice)	272
Lay's Chips packet	160
1 Bourbon Cream Biscuit	53
1 Marie Biscuit	26
1 scoop Vanilla Ice Cream	273
1 Ketchup sachet	13
1 tbsp Sugar	48
1 tbsp Honey	64
1 cup Coconut Water	46
1 Cadbury Dairy Milk Chocolate bar	200